PIE
ALL THE TIME

PIE
ALL THE TIME

Elevated Sweet and Savory Recipes for Every Occasion

TAYLOR HARBIN
Creator of All Purpose Flour Child

PAGE STREET
PUBLISHING CO.

PAGE STREET
PUBLISHING CO.

First published in 2021 by Taylor Harbin
Page Street Publishing Co.
27 Congress Street, Suite 105
Salem, MA 01970
www.pagestreetpublishing.com

Distributed by Macmillan, sales in Canada by The Canadian Manda Group.

25 24 23 22 21   1 2 3 4 5

ISBN-13: 978-1-64567-416-0
ISBN-10: 1-64567-416-9

Library of Congress Control Number: 2021930218

Cover and book design by Laura Benton for Page Street Publishing Co.
Photography by Taylor Harbin

Printed and bound in China

Page Street Publishing protects our planet by donating to nonprofits like The Trustees, which focuses on local land conservation.

To Mom and Dad

for making a home that nurtured my insatiable creative spirit and
for filling it with an endless love that encouraged it to grow.

And Avery

my first and biggest fan, always. I hope you never stop looking up to me,
and may I always be worthy of your gaze.

CONTENTS

INTRODUCTION

For me, baking has always been about two things: creating something out of thin air with my own two hands and the immense feeling of joy that comes from feeding people. Nothing is quite as satisfying as watching someone's face light up in delight after taking a bite of something I made for them. So why pie? Baking pies has always felt transcendent to me. I love the idea that, generations ago, it's the same activity my great-grandmother was doing in her own kitchen, and her mother before her and so on. And yet it's as relevant as ever today. Pie is timeless. And classic. And modern. It's endlessly adaptable and infinitely forgiving. It's sweet. It's savory. It's breakfast. It's dessert. It's an epic feast for a crowd. It's an after-school snack. It's the crowning jewel of a holiday fête. It's a casual, back-pocket secret weapon. In short: Pie is not one thing, but rather it contains a multitude of applications and occasions. It is the all-purpose, perfectly imperfect gift.

Let me take you back to how this book came to be in your hands. Growing up as an extremely introverted and creative kid, I was constantly looking for ways to express myself. I spent a lot of time drawing and painting, clay-molding and crafting and coating just about everything I owned in glitter glue and gel pen. When I discovered cooking, the whole world opened up for me. From the time I was old enough to climb up on a step stool, my mom gave me little jobs in the kitchen, such as snapping the ends off green beans, sprinkling cinnamon sugar on leftover pie dough and mashing bananas with a fork to make loaves of banana bread. When I graduated to making things on my own, I felt like I had really found my niche. I can very clearly remember attempting a complicated Martha Stewart dessert in the eighth grade: a watermelon bombe ice cream cake with many

intricate layers of different ice creams and sorbets. I was so full of pride when it turned out, I made my mom take my picture with it. The beaming grin on my face above my Abercrombie & Fitch T-shirt really said it all.

From then on, being in the kitchen is where I felt most at home and where my creativity knew no bounds; baking became my love language. I baked and decorated intricate sugar cookies for birthdays, fancy brûléed pumpkin pies for Thanksgiving, French macarons for friends' bridal showers, layer cakes and hand pies for work parties and even a wedding cake or two. As my skills in the kitchen grew, so did my confidence to experiment and create my own recipes. I played around with familiar flavors in new applications and put my spin on the classics. Needing a place to capture all my experiments and with a deep desire for a creative outlet, I started my blog, All Purpose Flour Child, in the fall of 2015, and it has been an adventure ever since.

In that same spirit of creating fun and unique recipes that explore new takes on familiar flavors, I set out to make this book, about my very favorite thing to bake, do just that. *Pie All the Time* is about exploring all that pie can be. There's the traditional, like my Wild Blackberry Birthday Pie (page 47) and Papa's Golden Pecan Pie (page 98). There are familiar classics reimagined into pie form, like Beef Bourguignon Skillet Pie (page 125) and Mocha Coconut Cream Pie (page 81), and even an updated and grown-up version of a classic childhood breakfast in the shape of Rhubarb, Ginger and Goat Cheese Pop-Tarts (page 139). It's also full of unique and inventive flavors, like Aperol Citrus Creamsicle Pie (page 66), Roasted Cherry Tomato Bloody Mary Galette (page 118) and Swedish Cardamom Roll Hand Pies (page 163), that will really show you just how versatile pie can be.

This book is a celebration of the seasons and the endless number of pies that can be made with just about any ingredient, any time of year and for any meal. For this reason, each chapter is arranged by season, so you'll always have a reason for pie. The recipes will take you through spring's best offerings, like candy-sweet strawberries, impossibly tart and bright rhubarb and the verdant vibrancy of snap peas. Summer unfolds into the very best of berries, the sweetest stone fruits, the juiciest summer tomatoes and even an ice cream pie or two. Fall, my favorite of the seasons, contains some real treasures starring juicy pears and honey—a fall crop for sure!—tart apples and many expressions of squash, from butternut to pumpkin. Winter is stuffed with cozy cranberry pies, comforting and warming stick-to-your-ribs classics and spices galore.

I'll share all my techniques for mastering the perfect crisp and flaky crust: no soggy bottoms! I'll melt away any worry or baker's anxiety you may have once harbored for making your own dough and show you it's really not so scary. No matter your skill level or pie-making experience, this is a book for all bakers. My hope for you and this book is that you find recipes you fall in love with and make over and over, until they become a part of your family, just as they are a part of mine. Happy baking!

Taylor

TOOLS, TECHNIQUES AND TIPS FOR PIE SUCCESS

Tools

Pie Pans

There's an endless variety of pie pans and plates to choose from, so how are you to know which is best? It all comes down to the material it's made of and how well it conducts heat. Most commonly, you'll find ceramic or stoneware, glass and metal. I've found that metal conducts heat best and yields a consistently crisp crust. Glass also does a great job of conducting heat, and you have the added benefit of peeking at the transparent bottom during baking, making glass a great option for beginner cooks to get comfortable with the timing and doneness of pies. Ceramic and stoneware conduct heat fairly well also, but, as pretty as some ceramic dishes may be, it's usually my metal or glass pan I reach for first. My favorite metal pans are made by USA PAN®. You can't go wrong with classic Pyrex® glass pans. Then there's size to consider. The recipes in this book call for a standard 9-inch (23-cm) pie pan, unless otherwise specified. A larger or smaller pan will affect not only the volume of filling the pie pan can hold, but also the way it bakes; it's always best to use the recommended size the recipe calls for.

Oven Thermometer

Oven thermometers cost only a few dollars, but they are a priceless necessity in your kitchen if you do any sort of baking. You'd be surprised how widely ovens range in temperature. My oven, for instance, is a good 25°F (14°C) off, so my oven thermometer allows me to adjust accordingly. It's also great for monitoring the temperature when you're taking things in and out of the oven and the temperature fluctuates. I prefer the style that clips or hangs from the oven racks, as you can easily see the temperature from the window of the oven, and you can leave it in the oven all the time.

Digital Kitchen Scale

I'll be completely honest with you: I did not consistently bake by weight until I started developing the recipes for this book. But as I've gotten into a regular routine, I find my measuring cups gathering dust on the shelf as I regularly reach for my scale. Weighing ingredients just makes so much more sense: It's much more accurate, but it's also easier and much less messy. Why I was ever intimidated by the scale, I'll never know. If you find yourself in a similar situation, let me release you from your worries, friend. Pick up a scale for yourself, tuck those measuring cups away and discover the freedom weighing ingredients will bring. I go for Escali brand, as the scales are affordable, reliable and accurate. And to all my international friends reading this: Have yourself a little chuckle, because you're already way ahead of us over here in the US.

A Quality Rolling Pin

Maybe you've been in a pinch on vacation making pizza or a pie and reached for a wine bottle in lieu of a rolling pin, and, for your ingenuity and resourcefulness, I salute you. But if you bake even occasionally, you really owe it to yourself to pick up a nice rolling pin. I have a few different styles and enjoy them all: a French pin, which is usually a fairly thin wooden pin with tapered ends, making it ideal for maneuvering dough; a silicone-coated pin with handles that honestly rolls dough out like a dream; and my most prized pin: a beautiful wooden one my dad made for my mom out of an old baseball bat when they were first married that's been passed down to me. The most important thing is selecting a rolling pin that feels right to you, not unlike selecting the perfect bowling ball.

Pie Weights

When blind-baking tart or pie crusts that will later be filled with things, it is essential to have something to hold the dough in place, hold its shape and keep it from puffing up while it par-bakes. You've got some options to choose from. But, personally, after extended use of both, I actually prefer something like uncooked rice or dried beans rather than fancy ceramic or stainless-steel pie weights. Not only are dried rice or beans more affordable, but I find the smaller size can fit better into the crevasses of a tart, filling out every nook and cranny. On the other hand, most pie weights are larger and bulkier and may be a bit clunky when using on something smaller or more delicate. But to each their own. While the dried rice or beans will no longer be fit to consume after you've blind-baked with them, they may be used as pie weights over and over. Let them cool, then tip them into a mason jar, pop a label on them and save them for your next baking project.

Bench Scraper

A good bench scraper is a great tool to keep around for scraping up bits of dough off your counter come cleanup time and for slicing doughs into portions or moving them around. You can get flexible plastic ones or more sturdy stainless-steel ones fitted with a wood handle. I have a few of each.

Ruler

When you're making something rather exact, such as a batch of pop-tarts®, it's nice to have a stainless steel or acrylic ruler you don't mind getting caked in flour. These can be picked up at any craft store.

Rimmed Baking Sheet

A rimmed baking sheet will be handy in any sort of scenario where there may be some leakage. The rims will protect the bottom of your oven, and you'll thank them for doing so. Just about every recipe in this book calls for you to either bake directly on one, such as a batch of hand pies or a galette, or placing your pie pan on top of one. This will not only help make pies easier to maneuver in and out of the oven, but also save a lot of mess later on. They're also endlessly useful for roasting vegetables and meat, toasting nuts and breads, making pizza and, of course, baking a pie. I like Nordic Ware, because they're high quality and don't warp but are still very affordable. It's nice to have at least a few in your collection as well. They come in several sizes, but I find the handiest ones are the quarter-sheet and half-sheet pans.

Microplane

This is certainly one of my most treasured tools in the kitchen. A nice sharp microplane grater is second to none when it comes to grating citrus zest, hard cheeses, such as Parmigiano-Reggiano or Pecorino Romano, and even grating spices like whole nutmeg or cinnamon sticks.

Techniques

Galette Folds

A galette, a French pastry, is nothing more than a rustic and freeform open-faced tart. Galettes may be filled with sweet or savory fillings. You may also see them called crostatas, which is essentially the Italian version.

Classic Fold-Over

This is probably the most common way to seal up a galette, and it's quite beautiful and effective. Simply fold the excess dough up onto the filling, overlapping it onto itself as you go to create a pleated pattern. There is no need to trim the dough or neaten up the edges, as the rugged look of the crust as it bakes adds to the rustic feel.

The Twist

This finish looks best when your dough has nice clean edges, so use a paring knife to run around the circumference of your dough after rolling it out to trim off any excess jagged bits. After you place your filling, pick a place on the dough to start and fold the dough back onto itself, right up against the filling. Pull the dough up and fold it back up onto itself again, right over the fold you just completed. Repeat around the rest of the filling.

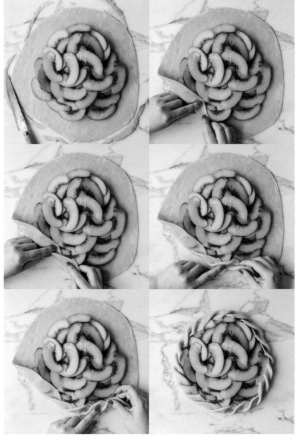

Scalloped Edge

Once you've rolled out your dough to the desired size and shape, use a 2-inch (5-cm) biscuit cutter or small glass. Press the outer half of the cutter into the edge of the dough, so that only half the cutter is making contact with the dough, and rock the cutter gently back and forth to make a cut. Continue around the whole edge of the dough, then go back and use a paring knife to separate any bits of dough the cutter didn't quite cut through. Fold up the dough around the filling.

Crimped Crust Edges

Crimping a pie serves a few purposes: It adds a beautiful decorative edge, but also helps to create a barrier for keeping fillings from spilling out and, in the case of double-crust pies, sealing the top and bottom crusts to prevent leaks.

Classic Finger Crimp

To create the classic finger crimp: create a "v" shape with your thumb and index finger on one hand and pinch the dough to create a "v" shape in the dough. At the same time, place your other thumb between the two fingers making the "v" and press down on the dough, adhering it to the pan. Continue around the rest of the pan until all the dough is crimped. You can go back and reshape any crimps that look uneven. Now, place your thumb and index finger each on the center of the crimp so that they're anchored at the point of the crimp. Take your other index finger, place it at the point where the two crimps meet and gently pull it back toward the center of the pie, exaggerating the shape of the two crimps. This is going to help the crimps keep their shape after baking, as the dough has a tendency to shrink and lose a bit of definition.

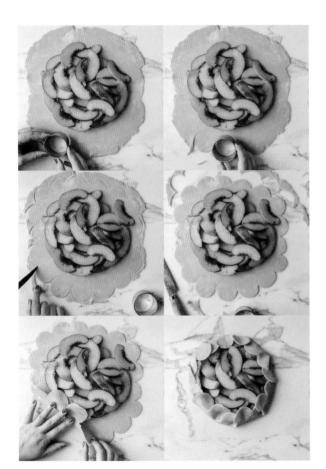

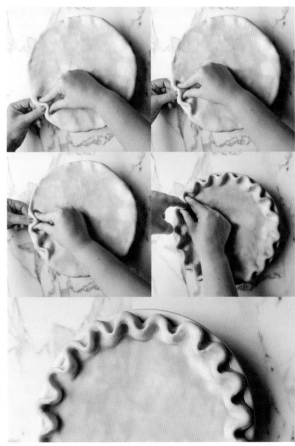

Fork Crimp

This simple method is great for beginners a bit intimidated by other crimping methods. It's also great if you're in a bit of a hurry. It requires nothing more than pressing the tines of a fork into the edges of the dough gently, to both adhere it to the pie pan and create a decorative design. To make interesting patterns, try experimenting with the angle of the tines when you press them into the dough.

Decorative Crust Edges

Braiding and twisting dough is really not unlike braiding hair, although fiddlier, as you have to take care not to tear the strands and the dough has a tendency to get warm quickly. Line a baking sheet with parchment paper before you begin. Decide how wide or narrow you'd like your twist or braid to be. Then, using a ruler and knife or pizza cutter, cut strips on your rolled-out top crust.

Twists

To make a twist, lay out one strip of dough, then place another on top and gently press the two ends together to join them. You can trim this portion off later, but it will help keep the twist or braid tight as you're creating it. Keeping the strips flat on your work surface, overlap them, alternating the strips, twisting the dough strips down as you go to create a twist, taking care to keep the strips close to each other with each time they overlap.

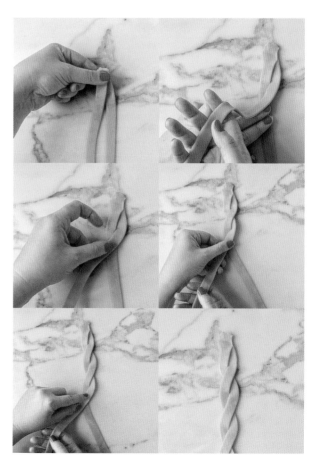

Pinch the other end of the strips together to keep the shape, then place the twist on the prepared baking sheet. To keep the dough cool, you can place the sheet in the freezer while you make other twists and braids.

Braids

Follow the same instructions to make a braid, adding one additional strip for a total of three. Alternate all three strips when twisting, just as you would when braiding hair. If you notice your dough getting too warm and hard to work with while you're making your twist or braid, simply pop it into the fridge for a few minutes to firm it up again.

These braids and twists may now be used in a lattice, used as the edge of a pie, as for the Honey-Cardamom Blueberry Slab Pie (page 48) or simply placed across the top of the pie, as for the Strawberry, Balsamic and Black Pepper Pie (page 36).

Double-Crust Topping Techniques

Classic Vents

For a double-crust pie, this is the simplest method to close up a pie. After rolling out the top crust to an inch (2.5 cm) or so larger than the pie pan, place it on top of the filling, then pinch the top and bottom crusts together to seal. Tuck the excess dough underneath itself and crimp the edges using your desired method. Cut about five or six 1- to 2-inch (2.5- to 5-cm) vent holes in the center of the top of the pie in a circular pattern to allow steam to escape.

Classic Lattice

This weave pattern is much easier to create than it looks. Start by rolling out your top crust to size, then use a ruler and a knife or pizza cutter to cut the dough into strips in whatever width you'd like. You can make each strip the same width or vary them to create a more interesting lattice.

Place strips across the top of the pie going all one direction, spacing them out as closely or as far apart as you'd like. For most lattices, I prefer a close-knit look, so I tend to leave just about ¼ inch (6 mm) of space in between. Now, turn the pie 90 degrees so that the strips are parallel. Starting at one end, fold back every other strip, then place down another strip, perpendicular to the ones on the pie. Reposition the strips that were folded back. You should now have the strip you just placed woven into the other strips. This time, fold back the opposite strips from what you folded last time. Place another strip down, and fold back the strips over it. Repeat this process of folding back the strips and placing another strip on top, alternating which strips are folded back each time another strip is added. Once your lattice pattern is complete, trim any excess from the ends of the strips so they're the same length as the bottom crust. Pinch the ends of the lattice together with the bottom crust to seal them, then tuck the excess dough underneath itself and proceed with crimping the edge however you'd like.

Once you get more confident with the lattice process, you can incorporate more elements into the weave, such as braids or twists, in place of some of the strips of dough.

Tips for Pie Success

Temperature

Temperature. Temperature. Temperature. When very cold butter hits a very hot oven, magical things happen. But there's a sad in-between too. A lukewarm crust gets very sad and droopy in the oven really quickly. This is why the freezer is our friend. Whether your kitchen runs a little hot or you just have hot hands, any time you're working with pie dough and you feel it getting too warm, feel empowered to throw it in the fridge or freezer for a few minutes to chill it down again. The aim is to have the coldest crust possible when it enters a hot oven. When the heat evaporates the water in the crust and the fat from the butter melts, it helps the dough to rise and create those flaky layers.

Frozen vs. Fresh Fruit

If I'm honest, I'm not the biggest fan of baking with frozen fruit most of the time, although I do make some exceptions on occasion. I think the fruit just tends to lose a bit of its integrity once frozen and will just never be quite the same as fresh. However, I know it's not always realistic to call for fresh fruit explicitly when I suspect many of us have a leftover bounty of spring's best rhubarb or some painstakingly hand-picked blackberries or blueberries kicking around the back corners of our freezers. So, if you must use frozen fruit, be sure to thaw it completely first, then drain it through a fine-mesh sieve to drain off as much excess water as possible before you proceed with your pie-making. Moisture is the enemy of pie-making, and, as the queen of home baking herself, Mary Berry, reminds us: "No one likes a soggy bottom."

What is Demerara Sugar?

Demerara is a less-processed cane sugar. It looks a bit like sanding sugar, but it's more amber in color and has light caramel notes. The texture adds a wonderful crunch to the edges of galettes and tops of pies and hand pies, but you can also substitute turbinado or raw sugar or even granulated sugar. I'd steer away from brown sugar, however, as the high molasses content causes the sugar to melt and burn rather than retain a granular shape in the oven.

Wait, No Vanilla Extract?

You'll notice as you make your way through the book that there's no mention of vanilla extract, only vanilla bean paste. That's because I truly believe the latter is superior to its extract counterpart in just about every way. Vanilla bean paste has a more intense vanilla flavor, with the added bonus of the inclusion of the vanilla seeds themselves, which equates to more flavor. The seeds also add an aesthetically pleasing visual cue in finished pies, similar to French vanilla ice cream. Vanilla bean paste provides the benefits of using a whole vanilla bean pod without the hassle of slicing it open and scraping out all the seeds. If you really prefer, vanilla extract can be substituted 1:1 for vanilla bean paste, but I'd encourage you to try swapping your usual extract with paste; I think you'll be pleasantly surprised. My absolute favorite is Heilala Pure Vanilla Paste, but Neilsen-Massey also makes a few great pastes, and that brand is widely available.

A STRONG FOUNDATION: THE DOUGHS

A house is only as strong as the foundation it's built on. Along the same vein, a pie is only as good as its crust, and good crust starts with good dough. I designed these dough recipes and the technique for making them be the easiest and most foolproof pie doughs you've ever made. There is no special equipment required. This is my promise to you: These doughs will yield the flakiest, crispiest crusts and be the perfect vehicle for whatever you choose to fill your pie with. Each dough is also made to be paired with sweet or savory pies, making them extra versatile.

While each pie is paired with a complementary dough recipe, many of them can be enjoyed with any number of dough variations. Many of the pies have an alternative dough suggestion, should you want to change things up and try a different version. Have fun and get creative!

ALL-PURPOSE DOUGH

While I love each and every dough recipe in this book, if I could only leave you with one, it'd be this. It's the foundation for all the rest and works for any sweet or savory pie you'd ever want to make. It's tender, flaky, crisp and sturdy. The egg yolks add richness but also keep the dough malleable and very easy to roll out and the vinegar helps create those flaky layers. Consider this recipe your back-pocket dough for any pie emergency that may come up.

YIELD

Makes enough for 1 large galette, a recipe of hand pies or a double-crust pie

INGREDIENTS

· 2 large egg yolks

· 2 tsp (10 ml) apple cider vinegar

· 4–6 tbsp (60–90 ml) ice water, or more, divided

· 2¾ cups (344 g) all-purpose flour

· 1 tsp sea salt

· 1 cup (224 g) unsalted butter, cold and cut into ½-inch (1.3-cm) cubes

CRACKED BLACK PEPPER VARIATION: Add 1 tablespoon (5 g) of freshly cracked black pepper to the flour mixture before adding the butter.

HERB VARIATION: Add 1 tablespoon (5 g) of roughly chopped fresh, hearty herbs, such as rosemary, thyme, sage or tarragon to the flour mixture before adding the butter.

PLANT-BASED VARIATION: Use a plant-based butter, such as Miyoko's Organic Cultured Vegan Butter, in place of the butter, skip the egg yolks and add another 1 to 2 tablespoons (15 to 30 ml) of ice water as necessary to bring the dough together. This variation bakes up a little paler than a crust made with dairy butter.

DIRECTIONS

In a small bowl, mix together the egg yolks, vinegar and 4 tablespoons (60 ml) of the ice water and set it aside. In a large bowl, combine the flour and salt. Add the butter pieces, and toss to coat them in the flour mixture. Using your hands, pinch the pieces of butter between your thumbs and pointer fingers to flatten them into thin shards. Continue until all the butter has been flattened, working quickly to prevent the butter from getting too warm.

Drizzle the egg mixture over the flour mixture, and toss the mixture with your hands to incorporate the ingredients. Drizzle over the last 1 to 2 tablespoons (15 to 30 ml) of ice water as needed, a little at a time, just until the dough comes together and is no longer dry and crumbly. You may not need all of the remaining 2 tablespoons (30 ml), depending on the humidity of the day, or you may need even a bit more. You want to add just enough water for the dough to feel firmly held together and smooth rather than dry and crumbly, but not so much that it's soft, wet and sticky to the touch.

Pat the dough out into a rough rectangle about an inch (2.5 cm) thick. Slice the rectangle into quarters, and stack the pieces on top of one another. Gently pat out the dough with your hands into a rectangle about an inch (2.5 cm) thick. Repeat the cutting and stacking once more. This process is going to give us all those flaky layers. Pat the dough into the size and shape called for according to the pie recipe instructions, wrap it tightly in plastic wrap and chill it in the fridge for at least 2 hours or, ideally, overnight. Allow the dough to sit at room temperature for a few minutes to soften slightly before rolling it out.

ABOUT PLANT-BASED OR VEGAN BUTTERS

Plant-based butters are not all created equal. A spreadable vegan butter will not work in this recipe. You'll need a firm, butter-like stick that you can treat as you would dairy butter, keeping it cold and cubed. In my tests, Miyoko's Organic Cultured Vegan Butter gave the best results. And it's also widely available and easy to find at a variety of stores.

BROWN BUTTER DOUGH

I won't lie to you. This dough requires a bit of additional prep time, but boy is it worth it. The depth that browned butter provides is unmatched. The nutty, rich flavors are a cozy complement for both sweet and savory pies. This dough has become a staple for many of my fall and winter baked goods. After you taste it, it will become a staple for you, too.

YIELD
Makes enough for 1 large galette, a recipe of hand pies or a double-crust pie

INGREDIENTS
· 1 cup + 2 tbsp (252 g) unsalted butter, cubed
· 1 large egg yolk
· 2 tsp (10 ml) apple cider vinegar
· 4–6 tbsp (60–90 ml) ice water, or more, divided
· 2½ cups (312 g) all-purpose flour
· 1 tsp sea salt

DIRECTIONS
In a saucepan over medium heat, melt the butter, then continue cooking it, swirling often to keep the milk solids from burning. Once the butter has melted, it will get foamy and bubbly. As the bubbles subside, it will brown quite quickly, so keep an eye on it. This will take 5 to 7 minutes, so be patient. As soon as the butter is a deep golden brown and is smelling nutty, immediately remove it from the heat and pour it into a bowl to stop the cooking, being sure to scrape in every brown bit, as they add quite a bit of flavor. Allow the butter to cool completely and solidify at room temperature. If your home is especially warm and you find it's taking quite a long time for the butter to solidify, you can pop the bowl in the fridge for a few moments; make sure not to leave it too long, or you won't be able to stir it. The butter will be separated at this stage, so we need to bring it back together. Using a wooden spoon or rubber spatula, stir the butter until it's one homogenous mixture. Transfer the butter to a piece of plastic wrap, parchment or wax paper, and wrap it tightly into a 3- to 4-inch (8- to 10-cm) log. Refrigerate the log to harden the butter completely. When you are ready to make the crust, cut the firm log into ½-inch (1.3-cm) cubes to use in the dough.

In a small bowl, mix together the egg yolk, vinegar and 4 tablespoons (60 ml) of the ice water, and set it aside. In a large bowl, combine the flour and salt. Add the butter pieces, and toss to coat them in the flour mixture. Using your hands, pinch the pieces of butter between your thumbs and pointer fingers to flatten them into thin shards. Continue until all the butter has been flattened, working quickly to prevent the butter from getting too warm. Drizzle the egg mixture over the flour mixture, and use your hands, in a tossing motion, to incorporate it. Drizzle over the last 1 to 2 tablespoons (15 to 30 ml) of ice water as needed, a little at a time, just until the dough comes together and is no longer dry and crumbly. You may not need all of the remaining 2 tablespoons (30 ml), depending on the humidity of the day, or you may need even a bit more. You want to add just enough water for the dough to feel firmly held together and smooth rather than dry and crumbly, but not so much that it's soft, wet and sticky to the touch.

Pat the dough out into a rough rectangle about an inch (2.5 cm) thick. Slice the rectangle into quarters, and stack the pieces on top of one another. Gently pat out the dough with your hands into a rectangle about an inch (2.5 cm) thick. Repeat the cutting and stacking once more. This process is going to give us all those flaky layers.

Pat the dough into the size and shape called for in the pie recipe instructions, wrap it tightly in plastic wrap and chill it in the fridge for at least 2 hours or, ideally, overnight. Allow the dough to sit at room temperature for a few minutes to soften slightly before rolling it out.

BUTTERMILK DOUGH

Buttermilk adds a wonderful, tangy flavor and brings an almost supple quality to dough. Pair this crust with sweet berry pies or rich savory pies for a special twist.

YIELD
Makes enough for 1 large galette, a recipe of hand pies or a double-crust pie

DIRECTIONS
· 2¾ cups (344 g) all-purpose flour

· 1 tsp sea salt

· 1 cup (224 g) unsalted butter, cold and cut into ½-inch (1.3-cm) cubes

· 7–9 tbsp (105–135 ml) buttermilk, cold, or more, divided

DIRECTIONS

In a large bowl, combine the flour and salt. Add the butter pieces, and toss to coat them in the flour mixture. Using your hands, pinch the pieces of butter between your thumbs and pointer fingers to flatten them into thin shards. Continue until all the butter has been flattened, working quickly to prevent the butter from getting too warm. Drizzle 7 tablespoons (105 ml) of the buttermilk over the flour mixture, and toss the mixture with your hands to incorporate the ingredients. Drizzle over the last 1 to 2 tablespoons (15 to 30 ml) of buttermilk as needed, a little at a time, just until the dough comes together and is no longer dry and crumbly. You may not need all of the remaining 2 tablespoons (30 ml), depending on the humidity of the day, or you may need even a bit more. You want to add just enough buttermilk for the dough to feel firmly held together and smooth rather than dry and crumbly, but not so much that it's soft, wet and sticky to the touch.

Pat the dough out into a rough rectangle about an inch (2.5 cm) thick. Slice the rectangle into quarters, and stack the pieces on top of one another. Gently pat the dough out with your hands into a rectangle about an inch (2.5 cm) thick. Repeat the cutting and stacking once more. This process is going to give us all those flaky layers.

Pat the dough into the size and shape called for according to the pie recipe instructions, wrap it tightly in plastic wrap and chill it in the fridge for at least 2 hours or, ideally, overnight. Allow the dough to sit at room temperature for a few minutes to soften slightly before rolling it out.

CHEDDAR DOUGH

This dough seems unassuming, but I promise you it's a sleeper hit. It's an obvious choice for savory pies, like a tomato and corn pie (page 111), but a total dark horse for a sweet fruit pie, like the Apple Cheddar Galette (page 56).

YIELD
Makes enough for 1 large galette, a recipe of hand pies or a double-crust pie

INGREDIENTS
· 1 tbsp (15 ml) apple cider vinegar
· 8–10 tbsp (120–150 ml) ice water, or more, divided
· 2½ cups (312 g) all-purpose flour
· ½ tsp sea salt
· ½ cup (113 g) unsalted butter, cold and cut into ½-inch (1.3-cm) cubes
· 6 oz (170 g) extra sharp cheddar cheese, grated

DIRECTIONS
In a small bowl, mix together the vinegar and 8 tablespoons (120 ml) of the ice water, and set it aside. In a large bowl, combine the flour and salt. Add the butter pieces, and toss to coat them in the flour mixture. Using your hands, pinch the pieces of butter between your thumbs and pointer fingers to flatten them into thin shards. Continue until all the butter has been flattened, working quickly to prevent the butter from getting too warm. Add the cheese, and toss to thoroughly coat it in the flour. Drizzle the vinegar mixture over the flour mixture, and toss the mixture with your hands to incorporate the ingredients. Drizzle over the last 1 to 2 tablespoons (15 to 30 ml) of ice water as needed, a little at a time, just until the dough comes together and is no longer dry and crumbly. You may not need all of the remaining 2 tablespoons (30 ml), depending on the humidity of the day, or you may need even a bit more. You want to add just enough water for the dough to feel firmly held together and smooth rather than dry and crumbly, but not so much that it's soft, wet and sticky to the touch.

Pat the dough into the size and shape called for according to the pie recipe instructions, wrap it tightly in plastic wrap and chill it in the fridge for at least 2 hours or, ideally, overnight. Allow the dough to sit at room temperature for a few minutes to soften slightly before rolling it out.

RYE DOUGH

I like to think of rye as a cooler version of whole wheat. Its hearty flavor and earthy, nutty—and even slightly sour—notes really stand up to rich, savory pies and give a bit of backbone to fruit tarts and pies.

YIELD

Makes enough for 1 large galette, a recipe of hand pies or a double-crust pie

INGREDIENTS

· 2 large egg yolks

· 2 tsp (10 ml) apple cider vinegar

· 8–10 tbsp (120–150 ml) ice water, or more, divided

· 2 cups (250 g) all-purpose flour

· 2 cups (200 g) rye flour

· 2 tsp (10 g) sea salt

· 1 cup (224 g) unsalted butter, cold and cut into ½-inch (1.3-cm) cubes

DIRECTIONS

In a small bowl, mix together the egg yolks, vinegar and 8 tablespoons (120 ml) of the ice water, and set it aside. In a large bowl, combine the all-purpose and rye flours and salt. Add the butter, and toss to coat the cubes in the flour mixture. Using your hands, pinch the pieces of butter between your thumbs and pointer fingers to flatten them into thin shards of butter, and toss them to fully coat the butter in the flour. Continue until all the butter has been flattened, working quickly to prevent the butter from getting too warm. Drizzle the egg mixture over the flour mixture, and toss the mixture with your hands to incorporate the ingredients. Drizzle over the last 1 to 2 tablespoons (15 to 30 ml) of ice water as needed, a little at a time, just until the dough comes together and is no longer dry and crumbly. You may not need all of the remaining 2 tablespoons (30 ml), depending on the humidity of the day, or you may need even a bit more. You want to add just enough water for the dough to feel firmly held together and smooth rather than dry and crumbly, but not so much that it's soft, wet and sticky to the touch.

Pat the dough out into a disc about an inch (2.5 cm) thick. Using a bench scraper or knife, slice the disc into quarters and stack the pieces on top of one another. Gently pat out the dough with your hands into a disc about an inch (2.5 cm) thick. Repeat the cutting and stacking once more. This process is going to give us all those flaky layers.

Pat the dough into the size and shape called for in the pie recipe instructions, wrap it tightly in plastic wrap and chill it in the fridge for at least 2 hours or, ideally, overnight. Allow the dough to sit at room temperature for a few minutes to soften slightly before rolling it out.

ANY-NUT DOUGH

Use most any nut you like for this dough; they add another layer of flavor to this easily adaptable dough for both sweet and savory pies. This dough is more fragile and prone to crack than all-flour doughs, so be gentle when rolling and handling it. If the dough happens to tear, you can easily press it back together.

YIELD
Makes enough for 1 large galette or a double-crust pie

INGREDIENTS
· 2 large egg yolks

· 2 tsp (10 ml) apple cider vinegar

· 4–6 tbsp (60–80 ml) ice water, or more, divided

· 1 cup roasted, unsalted whole nuts such as hazelnuts (133 g), walnuts (122 g), pecans (122 g) or almonds (160 g)

· 2¼ cups (281 g) all-purpose flour

· 1 tsp sea salt

· 1 cup (224 g) unsalted butter, cold and cut into ½-inch (1.3-cm) cubes

DIRECTIONS
In a small bowl, mix together the egg yolks, vinegar and 4 tablespoons (60 ml) of the ice water, and set it aside. In a food processor or high-powered blender, pulse the nuts until they are very fine crumbs but still have a bit of texture. In a large bowl, combine the nuts, flour and salt. Add the butter pieces, and toss to coat them in the flour mixture. Using your hands, pinch the pieces of butter between your thumbs and pointer fingers to flatten the butter into thin shards. Continue until all the butter has been flattened, working quickly to prevent the butter from getting too warm. Drizzle the egg mixture over the flour mixture, and toss the mixture with your hands to incorporate the ingredients. Drizzle over the last 1 to 2 tablespoons (15 to 30 ml) of ice water as needed, a little at a time, just until the dough comes together and is no longer dry and crumbly. You may not need all of the remaining 2 tablespoons (30 ml), depending on the humidity of the day, or you may need even a bit more. You want to add just enough water for the dough to feel firmly held together and smooth rather than dry and crumbly, but not so much that it's soft, wet and sticky to the touch.

Pat the dough out into a rough rectangle about an inch (2.5 cm) thick. Slice the rectangle into quarters, and stack the pieces on top of one another. Gently pat the dough out with your hands into a rectangle about an inch (2.5 cm) thick. Repeat the cutting and stacking once more. This process is going to give us all those flaky layers.

Pat the dough into the size and shape called for according to the pie recipe instructions, wrap it tightly in plastic wrap and chill it in the fridge for at least 2 hours or, ideally, overnight. Allow the dough to sit at room temperature for a few minutes to soften slightly before rolling it out.

CORNMEAL DOUGH

This dough is reminiscent of cornbread and is absolutely scrumptious in a sweet Blueberry Cornmeal Galette (page 51) or something ultrasavory like Chipotle Vegetable Chili Mini Pot Pies (page 164).

YIELD

Makes enough for 1 large galette, a recipe of hand pies or a double-crust pie

INGREDIENTS

· 2 large egg yolks

· 2 tsp (10 ml) apple cider vinegar

· 4–6 tbsp (60–90 ml) ice water, or more, divided

· 2 cups (250 g) all-purpose flour

· ¾ cup (128 g) finely ground cornmeal

· 1¼ tsp (6 g) sea salt

· 1 cup (224 g) unsalted butter, cold and cut into ½-inch (1.3-cm) cubes

DIRECTIONS

In a small bowl, mix together the egg yolks, vinegar and 4 tablespoons (60 ml) of the ice water, and set it aside. In a large bowl, combine the flour, cornmeal and salt. Add the butter pieces, and toss to coat them in the flour mixture. Using your hands, pinch the pieces of butter between your thumbs and pointer fingers to flatten them into thin shards. Continue until all the butter has been flattened, working quickly to prevent the butter from getting too warm. Drizzle the egg mixture over the flour mixture, and toss the mixture with your hands to incorporate the ingredients. Drizzle over the last 1 to 2 tablespoons (15 to 30 ml) of ice water as needed, a little at a time, just until the dough comes together and is no longer dry and crumbly. You may not need all of the remaining 2 tablespoons (30 ml), depending on the humidity of the day, or you may need even a bit more. You want to add just enough water for the dough to feel firmly held together and smooth rather than dry and crumbly, but not so much that it's soft, wet and sticky to the touch.

Pat the dough out into a rough rectangle about an inch (2.5 cm) thick. Slice the rectangle into quarters, and stack the pieces on top of one another. Gently pat out the dough with your hands into a rectangle about an inch (2.5 cm) thick. Repeat the cutting and stacking once more. This process is going to give us all those flaky layers.

Pat the dough into the size and shape called for according to the pie recipe instructions, wrap it tightly in plastic wrap and chill it in the fridge for at least 2 hours or, ideally, overnight. Allow the dough to sit at room temperature for a few minutes to soften slightly before rolling it out.

BUCKWHEAT DOUGH

Buckwheat, technically a seed and not a grain, is naturally gluten-free. Because of this, this dough, even though tempered with some all-purpose flour, tends to be a bit more fragile and needs to be handled with care. It has a unique and deeply earthy flavor with mild notes of bitterness. This crust complements pies with especially rich or cheesy fillings, like Havarti Dill Tartlets with Smoked Salmon (page 148), and sweet fruits or custard fillings like Papa's Golden Pecan Pie (page 98).

YIELD
Makes enough for 1 large galette, a recipe of hand pies or a double-crust pie

INGREDIENTS
· 2 large egg yolks
· 2 tsp (10 ml) apple cider vinegar
· 4–6 tbsp (60–90 ml) ice water, or more, divided
· 2 cups (250 g) all-purpose flour
· ¾ cup (102 g) buckwheat flour
· 1 tsp sea salt
· 1 cup (224 g) unsalted butter, cold and cut into ½-inch (1.3-cm) cubes

DIRECTIONS
In a small bowl, mix together the egg yolks, vinegar and 4 tablespoons (60 ml) of the ice water, and set it aside. In a large bowl, combine the all-purpose and buckwheat flours and salt. Add the butter pieces, and toss to coat them in the flour mixture. Using your hands, pinch the pieces of butter between your thumbs and pointer fingers to flatten them into thin shards. Continue until all the butter has been flattened, working quickly to prevent the butter from getting too warm. Drizzle the egg mixture over the flour mixture, and toss the mixture with your hands to incorporate the ingredients. Drizzle over the last 1 to 2 tablespoons (15 to 30 ml) of ice water as needed, a little at a time, just until the dough comes together and is no longer dry and crumbly. You may not need all of the remaining 2 tablespoons (30 ml), depending on the humidity of the day, or you may need even a bit more. You want to add just enough water for the dough to feel firmly held together and smooth rather than dry and crumbly, but not so much that it's soft, wet and sticky to the touch.

Pat the dough out into a rough rectangle about an inch (2.5 cm) thick. Slice the rectangle into quarters, and stack the pieces on top of one another. Gently pat out the dough with your hands into a rectangle about an inch (2.5 cm) thick. Repeat the cutting and stacking once more. This process is going to give us all those flaky layers.

Pat the dough into the size and shape called for according to the pie recipe instructions, wrap it tightly in plastic wrap and chill it in the fridge for at least 2 hours or, ideally, overnight. Allow the dough to sit at room temperature for a few minutes to soften slightly before rolling it out.

HANDLING YOUR DOUGH

HAND-MIXING IS BEST: There are many methods of bringing a pie dough together, but I prefer one in which I bring the dough together with my hands. I like the tactile quality of feeling the butter and flour in my hands, and I find I have much more control over the size of the butter shards when I make dough by hand. Large, thin shards of butter incorporated into the dough make for a flaky pie. If you prefer to make pie dough with a food processor or pastry cutter/blender, the dough recipes in this book will absolutely work with those methods. However, I'd encourage you to give it a try by hand at least once. I think you'll be impressed with the results. And, you'll have fewer dishes, too.

AHEAD-OF-TIME NOTE: One question I get asked often is, "Can I make my dough ahead of time?" I answer with an emphatic "Yes!" While you can definitely make your dough in as little as a few hours ahead of time, I'm a big fan of making my dough the day before and having it ready for me in the fridge when I put my pie together. One of the biggest favors you can do for yourself is to have a few extra discs of pie dough stashed in the freezer for a rainy day. Just be sure to label the dough and add the date, or it'll become an unidentified floating object in your freezer a year from now. Dough will keep in the fridge for about 3 days and in the freezer for 3 to 6 months, as long as it's sealed well to avoid freezer burn. In fact, when you're making a recipe from this book that calls for only a half recipe of dough, make a full batch and squirrel the other half away for a rainy day.

PREVENT STICKING: The enemy of rolling out the perfect crust is most definitely sticking, so don't be afraid to dust your work surface well. I usually grab a good palmful of flour, make a fist and tilt my hand sideways to spread the flour on my work surface evenly. Then, I'll lay the dough on top and sprinkle a bit of flour on top of the dough as well as the rolling pin, coating it. No matter the shape you're going for when rolling, it's a good idea to give the dough a scoot on the work surface after each pass of the rolling pin, so you keep it moving around. If you feel it start to stick anywhere, sprinkle a bit more flour underneath. To roll out a perfect circle, rotate the disc of dough a quarter turn after each pass of the rolling pin.

APPLY EGG WASH FIRST: When egg-washing and cutting steam vents, it's always best to egg-wash first, then cut any steam vents; otherwise, the egg wash can act as a sort of glue and seal the vents back up.

DARK EDGES: Should you notice the edges of your crust start to get dark while your pie is baking, but before your filling has set or the rest of the crust is dark enough, you can always add some foil to the edges. While there are all sorts of gadgets for protecting the edges of your crust from browning too much, I find foil just as effective, and my kitchen has one less one-trick pony taking up valuable real estate.

A FRUITFUL BOUNTY

A fruit pie: the quintessential vision of pie. Fruit pies are at once the perfect expression of the holidays and the symbol for the peak of summer. What to do with a bounty of fresh-from-the-orchard apples? Pie. Shoot, I bought an obscene amount of cherries because they just looked so darn good. Pie. Someone gifted me an entire basket of pears for Christmas, now what? Pie. I think you can see where I'm going. I'm always happy for an excuse to make a fruit pie. Just ask my dad, who gets one every year for his birthday—looking at you, Wild Blackberry Birthday Pie (page 47)—and occasionally on Father's Day, too. An apple pie is always a given for Thanksgiving, preferably with a deeply cheddary crust (page 56), and a Blueberry Cornmeal Galette (page 51) is always welcome as a last-minute need-to-take-a-dessert-to-this-thing recipe.

Inspiration strikes most often for me in concert with the seasons. With a new fruit in season practically around every corner, it's nearly impossible not to be excited. Come springtime, you can bet I'm making a juicy Raspberry Rhubarb Galette (page 35), with its honeyed sweetness and tart bite, as soon as I get my hands on some rhubarb, although it's actually technically a vegetable. And, can I also just tell you I'm a fruitaholic? If it was possible to OD on watermelon or strawberries, I probably would have done it by now. So, these recipes practically flew out of me. This chapter could've easily been twice as long, but that seemed unfair to the others. What you'll find in the following recipes are unique and inventive flavors for fruits of all seasons, so you'll never have to be without pie. I want only the best for you.

RASPBERRY RHUBARB GALETTE

I wait for rhubarb all winter long. I practically leap for joy at the first sighting of the magenta stalks at the farmers' market come springtime. Technically a vegetable, the extremely tart flavor in its raw state takes a bit of coaxing to transform it into something utterly special. A bit of honey and some fragrant raspberries manage to do just that in this gorgeous galette. The crispy, wholesome rye crust adds a bit of nuttiness and depth.

YIELD
Makes 1 (10-inch [25-cm]) galette

INGREDIENTS
· ½ cup (120 ml) honey

· Zest of 1 large orange, finely grated

· 1 tbsp (15 ml) freshly squeezed orange juice

· Big pinch of sea salt

· 1 lb (454 g) fresh rhubarb, about 6 large stalks, leaves discarded, cut on the bias into 2-inch (5-cm) chunks

· 1 lb (454 g) fresh raspberries, washed and dried

· 3 tbsp (27 g) cornstarch

· 1 recipe Rye Dough (page 26), patted into one large disc

· 1 large egg, lightly beaten

· Demerara or raw sugar

DIRECTIONS

In a large bowl, stir the honey, orange zest, orange juice and salt until combined. Add the rhubarb and raspberries to the honey mixture, and gently toss to combine the ingredients, being careful not to break up the raspberries too much. Sprinkle the cornstarch over the mixture, and toss to coat everything evenly.

Line a rimmed baking sheet with parchment paper.

Roll the dough out into a ¼-inch (6-mm) thick round, 12 to 13 inches (30 to 33 cm) in diameter, and transfer it to the prepared baking sheet. Add the filling to the center of the dough, leaving about a 2-inch (5-cm) border around all sides and reserving the juices left at the bottom of the bowl. Fold up the sides of the dough using one of the galette fold methods, such as the scalloped edge (page 15), around the filling. Drizzle the reserved juices over the top of the fruit. Freeze the galette for 30 minutes.

Meanwhile, preheat the oven to 400°F (204°C). Brush the sides of the dough with the beaten egg and sprinkle it with the demerara or raw sugar. Bake the galette for 50 to 55 minutes, until the filling is bubbling and the crust is a deep golden brown and crisp. Cool the galette completely before slicing and serving it.

VARIATION: Try this recipe with Buckwheat Dough (page 29).

HOT TIP: Be sure to cut away any trace of the leafy rhubarb ends, as they're poisonous if consumed.

STRAWBERRY, BALSAMIC AND BLACK PEPPER PIE

Strawberries and balsamic are a classic combination for a reason. The balance between candy-like strawberries ripened to perfection and the rich, acidic tang of balsamic vinegar just makes sense. The duo makes for a perfect pie filling, and the slightly spicy black pepper crust ties it all together for a decidedly unusual, yet lovely, spring pie.

YIELD
Makes 1 (9-inch [23-cm]) pie

INGREDIENTS
· 2¼ lbs (1 kg) fresh strawberries, halved or quartered if large
· ¾ cup (150 g) granulated sugar, divided
· 2 tbsp (30 ml) aged balsamic vinegar
· Pinch of sea salt
· ¼ cup (35 g) cornstarch
· 1 recipe All-Purpose Dough, cracked black pepper variation (page 22), patted into two discs
· 1 egg, lightly beaten
· Demerara sugar
· Cracked black pepper

DIRECTIONS
In a large bowl, toss the strawberries with ¼ cup (50 g) of the granulated sugar until they are well combined. Set aside the mixture to macerate for 1 hour, tossing the strawberries occasionally.

Strain the strawberries, and transfer them to a large bowl. You may discard the syrup or save it for adding to sparkling water or drizzling over oatmeal or pancakes. Add the remaining ½ cup (100 g) of granulated sugar, balsamic vinegar, salt and cornstarch to the strawberries. Toss well to combine the ingredients, then set aside the bowl while you prepare the crust.

On a well-floured surface, roll out one of the discs of dough to a ¼- to ⅛-inch (6- to 3-mm) thick round about 12 inches (30 cm) in diameter. Transfer the dough to a 9-inch (23-cm) pie pan, and position it so that it's centered with about an inch (2.5 cm) of dough hanging over the sides. Pour the filling into the pie pan. Roll out the second disc of dough, then choose your own adventure with how you'd like to crimp and close your pie (see pages 15–16). I chose to top mine with a combination of braids and twists (pages 16–17) but a lattice top (page 18) would be beautiful, too. Place the pie in the freezer for 30 minutes.

Meanwhile, preheat the oven to 425°F (218°C), and position a rack in the lower third of the oven. Line a rimmed baking sheet with foil. When the pie is ready to bake, place it on the prepared baking sheet. Brush the top with the beaten egg, and sprinkle it with the demerara sugar and black pepper.

Bake the pie for about 20 minutes, until the crust is matte and no longer glossy looking. Reduce the temperature to 400°F (204°C), and bake the pie for 35 to 45 minutes, until the crust is a deep golden brown color and the strawberry juices are bubbling and thick on top. If the edges are getting too dark before the rest of the crust is dark enough, wrap them lightly in foil to stop any further browning. Allow the pie to cool completely, so the juices thicken fully, before serving it; this will take several hours.

PISTACHIO FRANGIPANE AND PLUM TART

This tart, with its spiral of plums and pale green hue, is undeniably beautiful, but it's certainly not all style over substance. Tart, juicy plums are nestled into creamy, nutty and sweet pistachio frangipane, which caramelizes in the oven and takes on an almost chewy macaroon-like texture when baked.

YIELD
Makes 1 (12-inch [30-cm]) tart

INGREDIENTS
· ½ recipe All-Purpose Dough (page 22), patted into a disc
· 1 cup (144 g) shelled unsalted roasted pistachios
· ½ cup (100 g) granulated sugar
· ½ cup (112 g) unsalted butter, room temperature
· ½ tsp almond extract
· 1 large egg, room temperature
· 2 tbsp (16 g) all-purpose flour
· Pinch of sea salt
· 4 medium fresh black or yellow plums, halved, pitted and sliced into ½-inch (1.3-cm) wedges
· Powdered sugar, for dusting, optional

VARIATION: Try this recipe with Buttermilk Dough (page 24).

DIRECTIONS
Preheat the oven to 375°F (190°C). On a well-floured surface, roll the dough out into a ⅛-inch (3-mm) thick round, and transfer it to a 12-inch (30-cm) round tart pan with a removable bottom. Drape the dough down the side of the pan so as to not stretch out the dough. Using your thumb, trim away the excess dough by gently pressing the dough against the scalloped edge of the pan. Mark all over the bottom of the crust gently with the tines of a fork. Place the tart pan in the freezer for about 30 minutes, until the tart is very firm.

Line a rimmed baking sheet with parchment paper or foil. Cut a piece of parchment paper large enough to fit inside the pie shell and up the sides, with a few extra inches (8 cm) of overhang. Crumple up the parchment a few times to soften it. Smooth it out and fit it inside the pie shell. Fill up to the top of the pie with pie weights, dried beans or rice. Bake the tart for 20 minutes, until the dough is set and starting to get a little color on the edges. Remove the weights and parchment, and bake the tart for 10 minutes or so, until the crust is just light golden but still quite blonde. Cool the crust completely before filling it.

Meanwhile, make the filling. Pulse the pistachios and granulated sugar in a food processor until the pistachios are finely ground. In a medium bowl, combine the butter and pistachio mixture, and use a hand mixer or stand mixer fitted with the paddle attachment to beat the mixture until fluffy, a minute or so. Add the almond extract, egg, flour and salt, and whip again to combine. Pour the filling into the tart shell, and spread it into an even layer. Layer the plum slices on top in a spiral pattern, leaving a bit of room between each.

Reduce the oven temperature to 350°F (177°C), and bake the tart for 45 to 50 minutes, until the frangipane is set and has caramelized in places. Cool the tart completely before slicing and serving it. Dust the top with powdered sugar, if desired, when you are ready to serve the tart.

RUSTIC LAVENDER APRICOT TART

I'll admit lavender is one of those divisive flavors: you either love it or you hate it. It's definitely a delicate balance to achieve a hint of floral earthiness without going into soapy territory, but if you can get the balance right, as is the case with this tart, I think it's a magical addition. There's just enough lavender crushed into the sugar to know it's there, while letting the jammy apricots take center stage.

YIELD
Makes 1 (12 x 14–inch [30 x 36–cm]) tart

INGREDIENTS
· 1 tsp culinary grade dried lavender buds

· ½ cup (100 g) granulated sugar, divided

· 2 lbs (908 g) fresh apricots, about 8 large, pitted, halved and cut into ¼-inch (6-mm) slices

· Big pinch of sea salt

· 3 tbsp (27 g) cornstarch

· 1 recipe All-Purpose Dough (page 22), patted into one large rectangle

· 1 egg, lightly beaten

· Demerara sugar

· Honey Whipped Cream (page 175) or ice cream, for serving

DIRECTIONS
In a mortar and pestle, grind the lavender and 1 tablespoon (13 g) of the granulated sugar until the mixture is pulverized. This may also be done in a small food processor or spice grinder. Transfer the mixture to a large bowl and add the remaining 7 tablespoons (87 g) of the granulated sugar, the apricots, salt and cornstarch. Toss well to combine the ingredients, then set aside the mixture.

Line a rimmed baking sheet with parchment paper. On a well-floured surface, roll the dough out into a ¼- to ⅛-inch (6- to 3-mm) thick rectangle, about 14 x 16 inches (36 x 41 cm). Transfer the dough to the prepared baking sheet, and arrange the apricot slices in rows, layering them in a shingle pattern and leaving a 2-inch (5-cm) border along all sides. Fold the dough up over the apricots. Drizzle over any juices remaining in the mixing bowl. Freeze the tart for 30 minutes.

Preheat the oven to 400°F (204°C). Brush the sides of the tart with the beaten egg and sprinkle them with the demerara sugar. Bake the tart for 45 to 50 minutes, until the crust is a deep golden brown and the juices are bubbling. Serve the tart warm or at room temperature with the Honey Whipped Cream or ice cream.

VARIATION: Try this recipe with Rye Dough (page 26).

GIANT SPICED PEACH POP-TART

James and the Giant Peach *was a favorite book of mine growing up. The dreamy words of Roald Dahl painted a lush and idyllic picture, always leaving me feeling full of adventure and wonder. And really wanting a peach! To pay homage, I set out to create something as over the top and larger than life as the story is. And what's more fun than a giant pop-tart?! The filling is a lovely peach jam full of warm spices that's tucked into a buttery, crisp crust and is balanced with a sweet and tart glaze drizzled all over the top. This tart is equally delicious warm or at room temperature.*

YIELD
Makes 1 (9 x 12–inch [23 x 30–cm]) pop-tart

INGREDIENTS

Filling
- 1½ lbs (681 g) fresh yellow peaches, freestone if you can find them, peeled, halved, pitted and roughly chopped
- ½ cup (100 g) granulated sugar
- 1 tbsp (15 ml) freshly squeezed lemon juice
- 1 tsp ground ginger
- 1 tsp ground cinnamon
- ½ tsp ground cardamom
- Big pinch of sea salt
- 1 tbsp (8 g) cornstarch
- 1 tbsp (15 ml) water

Crust
- 1 recipe All-Purpose Dough (page 22), patted into two rectangles
- 1 egg, lightly beaten

Glaze
- ½ cup (63 g) powdered sugar
- 2 tsp (10 ml) freshly squeezed lemon juice
- ½ tsp vanilla bean paste
- Big pinch of sea salt

DIRECTIONS

For the filling, put the peaches, granulated sugar, lemon juice, ginger, cinnamon, cardamom and salt in a large, heavy-bottomed saucepan. Cook the mixture over medium heat, stirring occasionally, until the juices have reduced and the mixture has thickened, 30 to 40 minutes. Smash the peaches with a potato masher or the back of a large spoon until the mixture is about the consistency of chunky applesauce.

In a small bowl, combine the cornstarch and water. Stir the cornstarch mixture into the peach mixture, then allow the mixture to bubble and thicken, a minute or so. Remove the filling from the heat, and set it aside to cool completely.

For the dough, line a rimmed baking sheet with parchment paper. On a well-floured surface, roll out one of the rectangles of dough into a rectangle about ⅛ inch (3 mm) thick and 9 x 12 inches (23 x 30 cm) in size. Transfer the dough to the prepared baking sheet.

Spread the cooled peach mixture in an even layer on the dough, leaving a ½-inch (1.3-cm) border on all sides. Roll out the second rectangle of dough into the same size as the bottom. Brush the sides of the bottom crust with some of the beaten egg, place the second rectangle of dough on top of the filling, then press the edges on the beaten egg to seal them. Use a fork to crimp the edges together. Reserve the remaining egg for brushing on the top of the tart later. Freeze the tart for 30 minutes.

Preheat the oven to 400°F (204°C). Brush the tart with the beaten egg and cut a few vent holes in the top. Bake the tart for 45 to 50 minutes, or until it's a deep golden brown color. Cool the tart completely.

To make the glaze, whisk together the powdered sugar, lemon juice, vanilla bean paste and salt in a small bowl. The consistency should be quite thick, but still drizzly, like honey. Add a few drops of water, if necessary, to reach the desired consistency. Drizzle the glaze over the pop-tart. Let the glaze harden, about 30 minutes, then slice and serve.

VARIATION: Try this recipe with Any-Nut Dough (page 27), using walnuts.

SCRAPPY STONE FRUIT TART

Stone fruit is one of summer's most delicious offerings, but its delicate nature can lead to bruises and imperfections with practically a sideways glance. Show of hands for how many times you silently cursed the grocery store clerk for carelessly tossing your carefully selected peaches to the side as they rang you up. This tart offers a second chance to such rejected castoffs, which may be a little worse for wear but otherwise are perfectly delicious.

YIELD
Makes 1 (12-inch [30-cm]) tart

INGREDIENTS

· ½ recipe Rye Dough (page 26), patted into a disc

· ½ cup (120 ml) crème fraîche, room temperature

· 1 large egg, room temperature

· 1 tsp vanilla bean paste

· ½ cup (63 g) powdered sugar

· Pinch of sea salt

· 1½ lbs (681 g) ripe stone fruit, such as peaches, nectarines, plums, apricots or cherries, halved, pitted and larger fruits cut into ¼-inch (6-mm) slices

· ¼ cup (50 g) granulated sugar

· Zest of 1 medium lemon, finely grated

· 1 tbsp (9 g) cornstarch

DIRECTIONS

On a well-floured surface, roll the dough out into a ¼- to ⅛-inch (6- to 3-mm) thick round. Transfer the round to a 12-inch (30-cm) round tart pan with a removable bottom. Drape the dough down the side of the pan, so as to not stretch out the dough. Using your thumb, trim away the excess dough by gently pressing the dough against the scalloped edge of the pan. Mark all over the bottom of the crust gently with the tines of a fork. Freeze the tart shell for about 30 minutes, until it's very firm.

Line a rimmed baking sheet with parchment paper or foil, and preheat the oven to 400°F (204°C).

Place the tart shell onto the prepared baking sheet. Cut a piece of parchment paper large enough to fit inside the tart shell and up the sides, with a few extra inches of overhang. Crumple up the parchment a few times to soften it. Smooth it out and fit it inside the tart shell. Fill up to the top of the tart with pie weights, dried beans or rice. Bake the tart shell for 20 minutes, until the dough is set and starting to get a little color on the edges. Remove the weights and parchment, and bake the shell for 5 minutes, until it's light gold and matte.

While the crust is baking, prepare the filling. In a medium bowl, whisk the crème fraîche, egg, vanilla bean paste, powdered sugar and salt until combined. In another bowl, toss together the stone fruit, granulated sugar, lemon zest and cornstarch. Pour the crème fraîche mixture into the bottom of the tart shell, then pour the fruit mixture on top. Return the tart to the oven, and bake it for 50 to 55 minutes, until the filling is set and has almost no wobble when you jiggle the pan. Cool the tart before slicing and serving it.

VARIATION: Try this recipe with All-Purpose Dough (page 22).

WILD BLACKBERRY BIRTHDAY PIE

This is a classic blackberry pie, perfect in its simplicity and restraint. It is my dad's absolute favorite dessert in the world and, as he is the OG pie guy, he always requests only this on his birthday. Well, this pie and a '66 red Corvette, but we're still working on that one, Dad. He favors the tart flavor of wild blackberries and sometimes even marionberries, a Pacific Northwest blackberry hybrid, if we can find them. This pie is not overly sweet, relying on the perfectly in-season flavor of blackberries. It is a true celebration of the late summer berry, whether for a birthday or any old day. Pie over cake any day.

YIELD
Makes 1 (9-inch [23-cm]) pie

INGREDIENTS
- 2 lbs (908 g) fresh wild blackberries (see tip), washed and patted dry
- ¾ cup (150 g) granulated sugar
- Zest of 1 lemon, finely grated
- 1 tbsp (15 ml) freshly squeezed lemon juice
- 2 tsp (10 ml) vanilla bean paste
- Big pinch of sea salt
- ¼ cup (35 g) cornstarch
- 1 recipe Buttermilk Dough (page 24), patted into two discs
- 1 egg, lightly beaten
- Demerara sugar
- Honey Whipped Cream (page 175) or vanilla ice cream, for serving

DIRECTIONS
In a large bowl, toss to combine the blackberries, granulated sugar, lemon zest and juice, vanilla bean paste and salt. Sprinkle the cornstarch over the mixture, and toss again until the berries are evenly coated. Set aside the bowl.

On a well-floured surface, roll out one of the discs of dough to a ¼-inch (6-mm) thick round about 12 inches (30 cm) in diameter. Transfer the dough to a 9-inch (23-cm) pie pan, and position it so that it's centered with about an inch (2.5 cm) of dough hanging over the sides. Roll out the second disc of dough to the same size.

Pour the blackberry filling into the pie pan, top and crimp (pages 15–16) your pie using any method you'd like. Freeze the pie for 30 minutes.

Line a rimmed baking sheet with foil. Preheat the oven to 425°F (218°C) and position a rack in the lower third of the oven. When the pie is ready to bake, place it on the prepared baking sheet. Brush the top with the beaten egg, and sprinkle it with the demerara sugar. Cut a few vent holes on top to allow steam to escape.

Bake the pie for 20 minutes, in the lower third of the oven, then reduce the temperature to 400°F (204°C). Bake the pie for 35 to 45 minutes, until the crust is deep golden brown and the juices are bubbling and thick on top. If the edges are getting too dark before the rest of the crust is dark enough, wrap the edges lightly in foil to stop any further browning. Cool the pie completely before serving it with the Honey Whipped Cream or vanilla ice cream.

HOT TIP: If you can't find wild blackberries, regular blackberries work perfectly here as well. Wild blackberries tend to be a bit on the tarter side, so if your blackberries are especially sweet, you can decrease the granulated sugar by about ¼ cup (50 g) if you'd like.

HONEY-CARDAMOM BLUEBERRY SLAB PIE

Funnily enough, this pie was inspired by my favorite way to top my morning oats. I often make a quick compote of sweet blueberries, a touch of lemon, some honey and floral cardamom to add to oatmeal. It dawned on me this would make a killer pie, as the combination stands up to hearty oats much the same as it does enveloped in buttery crust. Enjoy this warm, with a scoop of vanilla ice cream or my Honey Whipped Cream (page 175), for a perfect after-dinner dessert or even on its own, for an indulgent breakfast. I won't tell if you don't.

YIELD
Makes 1 (9 x 13–inch [23 x 33–cm]) slab pie

INGREDIENTS
· 3 lbs (1.4 kg) blueberries, washed and dried

· ½ cup (120 g) honey

· Zest of 2 lemons, finely grated

· 2 tsp (10 g) vanilla bean paste

· 1½ tsp (5 g) ground cardamom

· Big pinch of sea salt

· ¼ cup plus 2 tbsp (54 g) cornstarch

· 1½ recipes All-Purpose Dough (page 22), patted into three rectangles (see tip)

· 1 egg, lightly beaten

· Demerara or raw sugar

DIRECTIONS

In a large bowl, toss to combine the blueberries, honey, lemon zest, vanilla bean paste, cardamom and salt. Sprinkle the cornstarch over the mixture, and toss it again to coat. Set aside the mixture.

Line a rimmed half-sheet pan with foil. On a well-floured surface, roll out the first rectangle of dough into about a 12 x 16–inch (30 x 41–cm) rectangle. Carefully transfer it to a 9 x 13–inch (23 x 33–cm) quarter-sheet pan and drape the dough down into it, so as not to stretch out the dough. You should have about ½ inch (1.3 cm) of overhang on all sides. Pour the filling in, and spread it in an even layer. Roll out the second rectangle of dough to ¼ to ⅛ inch (6 to 3 mm) thick, and place it over the pie. Press the top and bottom crust together to seal them, and trim any excess. Roll out the last rectangle of dough, create braids (page 17) and affix them to the edges of the pie, overlapping them. With a paring knife, trim any excess that may be hanging over the ends of the pan. Place the pan on the prepared half-sheet pan, and freeze it for 30 minutes.

Meanwhile, preheat the oven to 400°F (204°C), with a rack positioned in the lower third of the oven.

Brush the top of the pie evenly with the beaten egg. Cut a few large steam vents, then sprinkle the top evenly with the demerara sugar. Place the baking sheet in the lower third of the oven and bake the pie for 55 to 65 minutes, until the juices are bubbling and the crust is a deep golden brown. Allow the pie to cool before slicing it.

VARIATION: Try this recipe with Buttermilk Dough (page 24).

HOT TIP: For a simpler crust, just make one recipe of dough and crimp the edges of the dough with a fork instead of topping the pie with braided dough.

BLUEBERRY CORNMEAL GALETTE

Don't be fooled by this galette's short and unassuming ingredient list. The sweet, jam-like blueberry filling here is the perfect counterpoint to the soft and crumbly cornmeal crust, faintly reminiscent of cornbread. It's simple and satisfying and works equally well with thawed frozen blueberries you may have hanging around.

YIELD
Makes 1 (10-inch [25-cm]) galette

INGREDIENTS
· 2 lbs (908 g) blueberries, washed and dried
· ⅓ cup (73 g) granulated sugar
· Zest of 1 lemon, finely grated
· 2 tsp (10 ml) freshly squeezed lemon juice
· 2 tbsp (18 g) cornstarch
· Pinch of sea salt
· 1 recipe Cornmeal Dough (page 28), patted into one large disc
· 1 egg, lightly beaten
· Demerara or raw sugar

DIRECTIONS
In a large bowl, combine the blueberries, granulated sugar, lemon zest and juice, cornstarch and salt. Mix well to coat the blueberries evenly, and set them aside.

Line a rimmed baking sheet with parchment paper.

On a well-floured surface, roll out the crust into a ¼-inch (6-mm) thick round, about 12 inches (30 cm) in diameter. Transfer the crust to the prepared baking sheet, and pour the blueberry filling in the center, leaving about a 2-inch (5-cm) border of dough around all sides. Fold up the sides of the dough in a pleated pattern, following the instructions for the classic fold-over (page 14).

Preheat the oven to 400°F (204°C). Brush the sides of the dough with the beaten egg and sprinkle it with the demerara sugar. Bake the galette for 50 to 55 minutes, until the filling is bubbling and the crust is a deep golden brown. Allow the galette to cool before slicing and serving it.

SUMMER FRUIT CRUMBLE PIE

If you make only one pie this summer, let it be this one. Ripe stone fruit and tart berries sing together in harmony underneath a crispy, buttery layer of oat crumble. It would be perfect for any number of summer gatherings: idyllic picnics, casual backyard hangs and even festive 4th of July celebrations. Or just a random pie craving.

YIELD
Makes 1 (9-inch [23-cm]) pie

INGREDIENTS
Crust
· ½ recipe All-Purpose Dough (page 22), patted into a disc

Crumble
· 1 cup (125 g) all-purpose flour
· ½ cup (52 g) old fashioned rolled oats
· ½ cup (130 g) light brown sugar
· ½ tsp sea salt
· ½ cup (112 g) unsalted butter, cold and cut into ½-inch (1.3-cm) cubes

Filling
· 1 lb (454 g) ripe but firm yellow peaches or nectarines, freestone if you can find them, peeled, pitted and cut into ½-inch (1.3-cm) cubes
· 8 oz (227 g) fresh raspberries, washed and dried
· 8 oz (227 g) fresh blackberries, washed and dried
· ¾ cup (150 g) granulated sugar
· Zest of 1 lemon, finely grated
· 1 tbsp (15 ml) freshly squeezed lemon juice
· Pinch of sea salt
· 3 tbsp (27 g) cornstarch

For Serving
· Honey Whipped Cream (page 175) or vanilla ice cream

DIRECTIONS

For the crust, on a well-floured surface, roll the dough out to a ¼-inch (6-mm) thick round about 12 inches (30 cm) in diameter. Transfer the dough to a 9-inch (23-cm) pie pan, and position it so that it's centered with about an inch (2.5 cm) of dough hanging over the sides. Fold the excess under, and crimp the edges by pinching the dough between your thumb and index finger and pressing the dough down with your other thumb. Repeat around the rest of the pie. Freeze the crust for 30 minutes.

Meanwhile, preheat the oven to 425°F (218°C), and position a rack in the lower third of the oven. Line a rimmed baking sheet with foil.

Make the crumble. In a medium bowl, combine the flour, oats, brown sugar and salt. Using your hands, toss the butter to coat it with the flour mixture, then gently squeeze the butter into the flour mixture to form fists. Repeat until large clumps form. Crumble up the large chunks to form smaller pea-sized crumbles. Place the mixture in the fridge while you assemble the filling.

For the filling, in a large bowl, toss to combine the peaches or nectarines, raspberries, blackberries, granulated sugar, lemon zest and juice, salt and cornstarch. Pour the mixture into the prepared crust. Top the fruit with the crumb topping, spreading it into an even layer.

Place the pie on the prepared baking sheet, and bake it for 20 minutes. Reduce the temperature to 400°F (204°C), and bake the pie for 30 to 35 minutes, until the juices are bubbling and the crust and topping are deep golden brown. Allow the pie to cool completely before slicing it.

Serve the pie with the Honey Whipped Cream or vanilla ice cream.

VARIATION: Try this recipe with Buttermilk Dough (page 24).

GINGERY ROASTED PINEAPPLE COCONUT GALETTE

This tropical delight may just be the best vacation you take this year. Aromatic pineapple is roasted to perfection, coaxing out all its caramelly sweetness, and is tossed with a kiss of lime and fresh ginger for brightness and a hint of heat. The flaked coconut on top toasts in the oven as the galette bakes and is a perfect golden brown by the end. It's as delicious warm with some whipped cream or ice cream as it is room temperature the next day.

YIELD
Makes 1 (13 x 17–inch [33 x 43–cm]) galette

INGREDIENTS
· 1 large whole, fresh pineapple

· 2 tbsp (30 ml) melted coconut oil

· 2-inch (5-cm) piece fresh ginger, peeled and finely grated

· Zest of 1 lime, finely grated, plus more for serving, optional

· 1 tbsp (15 ml) freshly squeezed lime juice

· ⅓ cup (80 g) brown sugar

· Pinch of sea salt

· 1 recipe All-Purpose Dough (page 22), patted into 1 disc

· 1 egg, lightly beaten

· ½ cup (30 g) large flaked coconut, raw

· Demerara sugar

· Honey Whipped Cream (page 175) or vanilla ice cream, for serving

DIRECTIONS
Preheat the oven to 425°F (218°C). Cut the top and bottom off the pineapple, and stand it upright on a cutting board. Run a large knife from top to bottom, following the curve of the pineapple, to remove the peel. Slice lobes off either side of the pineapple, right up against the core. Repeat on the two remaining sides so that all you should have left of the center is the core. Cut each lobe into ¼-inch (6-mm) slices. On a rimmed baking sheet, toss the pineapple with the coconut oil to coat it. Arrange the pineapple in a single layer, and roast it until it is golden and caramelized, 25 to 30 minutes, flipping the fruit halfway through. Cool the pineapple to room temperature.

In a large bowl, stir to combine the ginger, lime zest and juice, brown sugar and salt. Add the pineapple, and toss to coat it evenly.

Line a rimmed baking sheet with parchment paper. On a well-floured surface, roll the dough out into a ¼- to ⅛-inch (6- to 3-mm) thick oval, about 13 x 17 inches (33 x 43 cm). Transfer the oval to the prepared baking sheet. Arrange the filling in the center, leaving about a 2-inch (5-cm) border on all sides. Fold up the dough around the filling. Freeze the galette for 30 minutes.

Meanwhile, preheat the oven to 400°F (204°C).

Brush the sides of the dough with the beaten egg, and sprinkle the coconut over the top of the egg wash, pressing the coconut lightly into the dough to adhere it to the egg wash. Sprinkle the demerara sugar over the top in between the coconut flakes. Bake the galette for 40 to 45 minutes, until the crust is deep golden brown and the coconut is toasted. Serve the galette warm, with Honey Whipped Cream or vanilla ice cream and a sprinkle of additional lime zest, if you'd like.

VARIATION: Try this recipe with Brown Butter Dough (page 23).

APPLE CHEDDAR GALETTE

At the tender age of nine, I was once served a slice of warm apple pie with a fat slice of cheddar cheese on top. I. Was. Mortified. Until I reluctantly took a bite. I'm not exaggerating when I tell you that bite was transcendent. Apple and cheddar are simply soulmates in any context, and, may I say, an extra cheddary crust enveloping sweet and acidic apples is a revelation. I get a raised eyebrow almost every time I serve this pie to first-time partakers. And, after they try it, people ask for seconds, along with all the leftovers and the recipe. But I'll let you be the judge.

YIELD

Makes 1 (10 x 12–inch [25 x 30–cm]) galette

INGREDIENTS

- 1½ lbs (681 g) apples, about 4–5, peeled, cored and thinly sliced (I like a mix of Gala and Granny Smith)

- 1 tsp freshly squeezed lemon juice

- 3 tbsp (23 g) all-purpose flour

- ½ cup (100 g) granulated sugar, or more or less, depending on the sweetness of the apples

- 1 tsp ground cinnamon

- Big pinch of sea salt

- 1 recipe Cheddar Dough (page 25), patted into one large rectangle

- 1 egg, lightly beaten

- Demerara sugar

DIRECTIONS

In a large bowl, toss the apples with the lemon juice to coat them, then add the flour, granulated sugar, cinnamon and salt and toss to coat. Set aside the apples.

Line a rimmed baking sheet with parchment paper. On a well-floured surface, roll the dough out into a ¼- to ⅛-inch (6- to 3-mm) thick rectangle, about 14 x 16 inches (36 x 41 cm). Transfer the dough to the prepared baking sheet. Spread the apples in an even layer over the dough, leaving a 2-inch (5-cm) border around all sides. Fold up the sides of the dough over the apples and gently press it into place. Freeze the galette for 30 minutes.

Preheat the oven to 400°F (204°C). Brush the dough with the beaten egg and sprinkle it with the demerara sugar. Bake the galette for 45 to 50 minutes, until the crust is very deep golden brown and the filling is bubbling and thick. Cover the top of the galette with foil, if necessary, if the dough is browning in places too quickly. Cool the galette slightly before serving it.

CARAMELIZED HONEY AND GINGER PEAR PIE

My uncle Tom keeps his own bees and, each fall, he harvests honey for the year. The yield is always impressive, especially with having only a few hives, but it is still revered as a precious commodity. Everyone in our family gets a jar and, let me tell you, that stuff is like gold. You better savor it because once it's gone, you'll have to wait another year for it to come around again. If you've never tried real-deal local honey, I highly encourage you to find a local beekeeper at your farmers' market. And if you've never had caramelized honey, it's a real treat. By caramelizing it, we're coaxing out all sorts of toasty notes and adding depth of flavor and interest to the honey. It's quite simple, yet transforms the whole pie, as the flavor complements the sweet pears so well. The spicy ginger offsets the sweetness and really drives home all the flavors.

YIELD
Makes 1 (9-inch [23-cm]) pie

INGREDIENTS
· ¾ cup (180 ml) honey
· 2 lbs (908 g) ripe but firm Anjou or Bartlett pears, about 6 medium, peeled, cored and cut into ¼-inch (6-mm) slices
· 1½ tsp (8 g) finely grated fresh ginger
· ½ tsp ground cinnamon
· 3 tbsp (27 g) cornstarch
· Pinch of sea salt
· 1 recipe Brown Butter Dough (page 23), patted into two discs
· 1 egg, lightly beaten
· Demerara sugar
· Honey Whipped Cream (page 175) or vanilla ice cream, for serving

DIRECTIONS

In a small saucepan, cook the honey over medium-low heat without stirring it; rather, swirl the pan until the mixture starts to gently bubble. Continue cooking until the honey has darkened in color to a deep amber and smells toasty and caramelized, 3 to 5 minutes. If the honey starts to bubble up too much, you can take it off the heat for a moment until the bubbling subsides, then return it to the heat. Remove the honey from the heat and let it cool completely.

In a large bowl, stir to combine the pears, ginger, cinnamon, cornstarch, salt and cooled caramelized honey, being careful not to break up the pears. Set aside the mixture.

On a well-floured surface, roll out one of the discs of dough to a ¼- to ⅛-inch (6- to 3-mm) thick round about 12 inches (30 cm) in diameter. Transfer the dough to a 9-inch (23-cm) pie pan, and position it so that it's centered with about an inch (2.5 cm) of dough hanging over the sides. Roll out the second disc of dough to the same size. Pour the filling into the pie pan, and top and crimp (pages 15–16) your pie using any method you'd like. Freeze the pie for 30 minutes.

Line a rimmed baking sheet with foil. Preheat the oven to 425°F (218°C), and position a rack in the lower third of the oven.

When the pie is ready to bake, place it on the prepared baking sheet. Brush the top with the beaten egg and sprinkle it with the demerara sugar. Cut a few vent holes on top to allow steam to escape, unless you've topped the pie with a lattice. Bake the pie in the lower third of the oven for 20 minutes. Reduce the oven temperature to 400°F (204°C), and bake the pie for 35 to 45 minutes, until the crust is deep golden brown and the juices are bubbling and thick on top. If the edges are getting too dark before the rest of the crust is dark enough, wrap them lightly in foil to stop any further browning.

Allow the pie to cool completely for several hours before serving it, with the Honey Whipped Cream or vanilla ice cream.

MULLING SPICE APPLE RYE PANDOWDY

The aroma of this pie alone is enough to send droves of neighbors pounding down your door demanding to know what's in the oven. The flavors are reminiscent of heady spices and sweet mulled cider on a crisp fall day, citrusy and rich hot toddies and a classic apple pie. My parents have a mini apple orchard in their backyard, and there's nothing I love more than heading down the hill to pluck a few for the first harvest when fall rolls around. This recipe has become a favorite, as it really lets the apples take center stage. I like to think of a pandowdy as the pie version of a cobbler. There's lots of luscious filling and a crispy pie top, often in bits and pieces rather than a single lid. No bottoms, just the top, like Winnie-the-Pooh.

YIELD

Makes 1 (10-inch [25-cm]) pandowdy

INGREDIENTS

- ½ recipe Rye Dough (page 26), patted into a disc
- 3 lbs (1.4 kg) apples, about 8–9, peeled, cored and cut into ¼-inch (6-mm) slices (I like a mix of Gala and Granny Smith)
- ⅔ cup (160 g) light brown sugar
- 3 tbsp (24 g) all-purpose flour
- Zest of 1 orange, finely grated
- 3 tbsp (45 ml) rye whiskey (see tip)
- Big pinch of sea salt
- 1 tsp ground cinnamon
- ½ tsp ground ginger
- ¼ tsp ground cloves
- 1 egg, lightly beaten
- Demerara sugar
- Honey Whipped Cream (page 175) or ice cream, for serving

DIRECTIONS

Preheat the oven to 400°F (204°C), and line a baking sheet with parchment paper.

On a well-floured work surface, roll out the dough into a ¼- to ⅛-inch (6- to 3-mm) thickness. Use a small cookie cutter or biscuit cutter to cut out small shapes, and lay them in a single layer on the prepared baking sheet. Place the baking sheet in the fridge while you make the filling.

In a large bowl, stir to combine the apples, brown sugar, flour, orange zest, whiskey, salt, cinnamon, ginger and cloves. Pour the mixture into a 10-inch (25-cm) cast-iron or ovenproof skillet. It will look like too many apples, but they'll cook down quite a bit. Use your hands to jigsaw them into even layers and make the top a fairly flat layer, as this will make it easier to place the dough pieces on top. Pull the baking sheet out of the fridge and arrange the dough pieces in a haphazard pattern, shingling the bits of dough so they overlap a bit on the top of the apple filling. Be sure the filling is covered. Brush the dough with the beaten egg, and sprinkle it with the demerara sugar.

Place the skillet on the prepared baking sheet, and bake the pandowdy for 50 to 55 minutes, until the filling is bubbling and the crust is deep golden brown. Cool the pandowdy completely before serving it with the Honey Whipped Cream or ice cream.

HOT TIP: If you can't find rye whiskey but you have a favorite whiskey or bourbon around, feel free to use that instead.

THINK SCRAPPY! Have some leftover dough scraps? Put them to good use with a recipe from the Waste Not, Want Not chapter (page 181).

CRANBERRY SAGE SLAB PIE

Cranberries are oft overlooked as a stand-alone pie fruit and take on the supporting role on our holiday tables, usually in the shape of a can, if you catch my drift. And that's a shame, because their bright, tart flavor offers a welcome addition to rich, buttery crust and earthy sage. The slab pie form offers a nice ratio of crust to fruit and is ideal for traveling to your Friendsgiving gathering or Grandma's house.

YIELD
Makes 1 (9 x 13–inch [23 x 33–cm]) slab pie

INGREDIENTS
· 48 oz (1.4 kg) fresh cranberries, washed and dried, or thawed frozen cranberries

· 1 cup (260 g) brown sugar

· Zest of 1 medium orange, finely grated

· 2 tbsp (30 ml) freshly squeezed orange juice

· 1 tsp ground cinnamon

· 1 tbsp (3 g) finely chopped fresh sage

· Big pinch of sea salt

· 2 tbsp (18 g) cornstarch

· 1 recipe All-Purpose Dough, herb variation with sage (page 22), patted into two rectangles

· 1 egg, lightly beaten

· Demerara or raw sugar

· Honey Whipped Cream (page 175) or ice cream, for serving

DIRECTIONS

In a large bowl, toss to combine the cranberries, brown sugar, orange zest and juice, cinnamon, sage and salt. Sprinkle the cornstarch over the mixture, toss it again to coat and set it aside.

Line a rimmed half-sheet pan with foil.

On a well-floured surface, roll out the first rectangle of dough out into a 12 x 16–inch (30 x 41–cm) rectangle. Carefully transfer it to a 9 x 13–inch (23 x 33–cm) rimmed quarter-sheet pan, and drape the dough down into it, so as not to stretch out the dough. You should have about ½ inch (1.3 cm) of overhang on all sides. Pour the filling on top of the dough, then spread it in an even layer.

Roll out the second rectangle of dough to ¼ to ⅛ inch (6 to 3 mm) thick. Top and crimp (pages 15–16) your pie using any method. Place the pie on the prepared half-sheet pan, and freeze it for 30 minutes.

Meanwhile, preheat the oven to 400°F (204°C) with a rack positioned in the lower third of the oven. Brush the top of the pie evenly with the beaten egg. Cut a few large steam vents, unless you've used a lattice top, and sprinkle the crust evenly with the demerara sugar. Place the baking sheet in the lower third of the oven and bake the pie for 55 to 60 minutes, until the juices are bubbling and the crust is a deep golden brown.

Cool the pie before slicing it and serving it, with the Honey Whipped Cream or ice cream.

CUSTARDS AND CURDS AND MERINGUES, OH MY!

This chapter, full of creamy concoctions, is a triumphant expression of cloud-like textures and smoother-than-silk layers of tangy, tart and rich fillings. I wasn't always appreciative of these sorts of desserts. To be honest, cream and meringue pies once conjured up images of retro cookbooks with unnaturally neon illustrations of sky-high desserts made with Jell-O, marshmallow fluff and canned fruits, so I never really saw the appeal. But one slice of creamy and tart lemon meringue pie changed everything for me. The combination of shatteringly crisp and buttery crust, the creamy and sharp bite of the lemon curd and the velvety, marshmallow-like meringue was a revelation. When I set out to make my own version, I turned to one of my favorite cocktails to draw inspiration and created the Paloma Meringue Pie (page 70). The result is a layer of salty-sweet, super tangy grapefruit and tequila-spiked curd, tucked into a perfect crust and covered in a cloud of meringue.

This chapter has something for everyone to love and appreciate. If you're a chocolate fiend, the Frozen Minty Malted Grasshopper Tart (page 75) and Rosemary Dark Chocolate Ganache Tart (page 84) are not to be missed. If you want something ultrarich and practically no-bake, the Honey Tahini Mousse Tart (page 73) will become a favorite. And for all of my traditional peeps: I got you, too. Papa's Golden Pecan Pie (page 98) and the Salted Caramel Pumpkin Tart (page 97) are just waiting to become holiday favorites. Whether you're an old pro or a baking novice, I hope these recipes help take away any fears you may have and build your confidence. You can do it!

APEROL CITRUS CREAMSICLE PIE

What do you get when you cross a key lime pie, a creamsicle® and an Aperol spritz? This pie. By far my favorite summer cocktail, I often imbibe the pleasantly bitter aperitif alongside a splash of citrus juice. I wanted to find a way to distill that flavor in a pie. Since Aperol pairs so nicely with bright citrus, it seemed only natural to spike a traditional cream pie with a bit. The result is a rich and creamy creamsicle pie with a grown-up flavor profile. Cin cin.

YIELD
Makes 1 (9-inch [23-cm]) pie

INGREDIENTS
Crust
· 6 tbsp (84 g) unsalted butter
· ¼ cup (60 ml) honey
· 8 oz (227 g) graham crackers (1½ sleeves)
· Pinch of sea salt

Filling
· 4 large egg yolks
· Zest of 1 large orange, finely grated
· Zest of 1 large lemon, finely grated
· ¼ cup (60 ml) freshly squeezed orange juice
· 2 tbsp (30 ml) freshly squeezed lemon juice
· 1 (14-oz [396-g]) can sweetened condensed milk
· ¼ cup (60 ml) Aperol

For Serving
· ½ cup (65 g) Honey Whipped Cream (page 175)
· Finely grated orange zest

DIRECTIONS

For the crust, preheat the oven to 350°F (177°C). In a small saucepan over medium-low heat, melt the butter. Once melted, remove the pan from the heat, and stir in the honey. Set aside the pan.

In a food processor, pulse the graham crackers until they resemble fine breadcrumbs. Transfer the crumbs to a large bowl, and stir in the butter and honey mixture and salt. Mix until the ingredients are well combined and the mixture is clumpy. Transfer the crumbs to a 9-inch (23-cm) pie pan, and press the mixture into the bottom and sides evenly, using a glass or round measuring cup to press the crumbs evenly around all the sides and pressing down on the bottom to ensure the crust is firmly pressed into the whole pan.

Bake the crust for 10 to 12 minutes, until it's golden brown and smells toasty. If the bottom puffs up a bit during baking, just gently press it back down again with the bottom of a glass or measuring cup once it's finished baking. Cool the crust completely before filling it.

Meanwhile, make the filling. In a large bowl, use an electric mixer to whisk the egg yolks until they are thick and pale, about 2 minutes. Add the orange and lemon zest, the orange and lemon juice, sweetened condensed milk and Aperol; mix again until the ingredients are well-combined. Pour the filling into the cooled crust.

Bake the pie for 15 to 20 minutes, until the filling is set and no longer wobbles when you jiggle the pan. Allow the pie to cool to room temperature, then transfer it to the fridge and chill it for at least 4 hours or up to overnight.

To serve the pie, fill a small piping bag or resealable plastic bag fitted with a star tip with the whipped cream. Pipe six small rosettes around the edge of the pie, about an inch (2.5 cm) apart. Alternatively, simply dollop the whipped cream on top with a spoon. Top each rosette with a bit of the orange zest. Serve the pie immediately.

CORIANDER LIME TART

This tart takes the idea of lemon bars and turns it on its head. The rich, custardy lime filling is mouth-puckering and sweet all at once, and is perfectly balanced by the tender, buttery shortbread crust. The coriander seeds add a wonderful hint of savory earthiness that pairs beautifully with the simultaneously sharp and sweet lime filling.

YIELD
Makes 1 (12-inch [30-cm]) tart

INGREDIENTS
Crust
- 1½ cups (187 g) all-purpose flour
- 2 tbsp (18 g) cornstarch
- ⅓ cup (64 g) granulated sugar
- ½ tsp sea salt
- 10 tbsp (143 g) unsalted butter, melted and cooled

Filling
- 3 tbsp (28 g) finely grated lime zest, from about 6 large limes
- ¾ cup (180 ml) freshly squeezed lime juice, from about 6–8 large limes
- 1½ cups (300 g) granulated sugar
- 1 tsp sea salt
- 4 large eggs, room temperature
- 1 tsp vanilla bean paste
- ¼ cup (31 g) all-purpose flour
- 3 tsp (8 g) coriander seeds, crushed

DIRECTIONS
For the crust, preheat the oven to 350°F (177°C). In a bowl, whisk to combine the flour, cornstarch, sugar and salt. Pour in the melted butter, and stir the mixture well to combine the ingredients. Transfer the mixture to a 12-inch (30-cm) tart pan with a removable bottom. Using your hands, press the mixture into the bottom and sides evenly. It will look like there's not enough, but there is! I find it's easiest to start pressing the sides evenly first, then evenly distribute the remaining dough on the bottom. Place the tart on a rimmed baking sheet, and bake it for 20 to 25 minutes, until golden brown. If the bottom puffs up a bit during baking, just gently press it back down again with the bottom of a glass or measuring cup once it's finished baking.

Make the filling while the crust bakes. In a large bowl, whisk to combine well the lime zest and juice, sugar, salt, eggs, vanilla bean paste, flour and coriander. Pour the filling into the tart shell. Carefully slide the baking sheet back into the oven, taking care not to spill the filling. Bake the tart for 30 to 35 minutes, until the filling has set but has a slight wobble in the center. Cool the tart completely before serving it.

PALOMA MERINGUE PIE

This fun spin on a classic citrus meringue pie borrows inspiration from the paloma cocktail with the use of fragrant grapefruit and lime, along with a splash of tequila for a truly over-the-top pie. The creamy, wobbly filling sits nicely inside the buttery crust, baked to crisp perfection, and then is topped with golden-torched marshmallow-like meringue.

YIELD
Makes 1 (9-inch [23-cm]) pie

INGREDIENTS
Crust
- ½ recipe All-Purpose Dough (page 22), patted into a disc
- 1 large egg, lightly beaten

Filling
- ¼ cup (35 g) cornstarch
- 1 cup (200 g) granulated sugar
- 2 tsp (4 g) freeze-dried raspberry powder, optional (see tip)
- 1 tsp sea salt
- 4 large egg yolks
- 1¼ cups (300 ml) water
- ¾ cup (180 ml) freshly squeezed grapefruit juice, from about 2 medium grapefruits
- 2 tbsp (30 ml) freshly squeezed lime juice, from about 1 medium lime
- Zest of 1 large grapefruit, finely grated
- Zest of 1 large lime, finely grated
- 4 tbsp (56 g) unsalted butter, room temperature, cut into small pieces
- ¼ cup (60 ml) silver tequila

Meringue
- 4 large egg whites, room temperature
- 1 cup (200 g) granulated sugar
- ¼ tsp cream of tartar
- ¼ tsp sea salt
- 1 tsp vanilla bean paste
- Flaky salt

DIRECTIONS
For the crust, preheat the oven to 425°F (218°C). On a well-floured surface, roll the dough out to a ¼-inch (6-mm) thick round about 12 inches (30 cm) in diameter. Transfer the dough to a 9-inch (23-cm) pie pan, and position it so that it's centered with about an inch (2.5 cm) of dough hanging over the sides. Tuck the excess dough underneath itself. Crimp the edges by pinching the dough between your thumb and index finger, and press the dough between those fingers with your other thumb, pressing down slightly to adhere the edge of the dough to the pan. Repeat around the whole edge. Prick the bottom of the dough all over with a fork, and freeze the crust for 30 minutes.

Line a rimmed baking sheet with parchment paper or foil. To blind-bake the crust, cut a piece of parchment paper large enough to fit inside the pie shell and up the sides with a few extra inches of overhang. Crumple up the parchment a few times to soften it. Smooth it out and fit it inside the pie shell. Fill the parchment up to the top of the pie with pie weights, dried beans or rice. Transfer the crust to the prepared baking sheet, and bake it for 20 minutes, until the crust is just set. Remove the weights by lifting out the whole piece of parchment.

(continued)

PALOMA MERINGUE PIE (CONTINUED)

Reduce the temperature of the oven to 350°F (177°C). Brush the crust all over the bottom and sides lightly with the egg wash, and bake it for 30 to 35 minutes, or until the crust is a deep golden brown and is crisp. The egg wash will help seal the crust and prevent it from becoming soggy once it's filled with the grapefruit filling. Wrap the crimped edges lightly in foil if they're getting too brown before the bottom has crisped properly. Cool the crust completely before filling it.

Make the filling while the crust bakes. In a medium saucepan, whisk together the cornstarch, sugar, raspberry powder, if using, and salt. Add the egg yolks, water, grapefruit juice and lime juice and whisk vigorously to combine. Bring the mixture to a simmer over medium heat and cook it for 10 to 12 minutes until the mixture has thickened, whisking constantly. The full thickening power of cornstarch is only activated at the boiling point, so be sure the mixture is really simmering.

Remove the pan from the heat and add the grapefruit zest, lime zest and butter; whisk to combine. Finally, whisk in the tequila. Pour the mixture into the cooled pie shell and chill the pie for about 2 hours and up to overnight, or until it's very firm.

Make the meringue the day you are serving the pie. Bring a few inches of water to a simmer in a saucepan. In the bowl of a stand mixer, place the egg whites, sugar, cream of tartar and salt. Rest the bowl over the simmering water, being sure it does not make direct contact with the water. Whisk often until the sugar has completely dissolved and the mixture is warm, 8 to 10 minutes. You should be able to rub the mixture between your fingers without feeling any grit from the sugar. If you do, keep whisking over the heat until the sugar is completely dissolved. Transfer the bowl to the stand mixer and beat the mixture on high, using the whisk attachment, until the mixture is thick, white and glossy, about 5 minutes or so. The mixture is ready when it holds stiff peaks. Add the vanilla bean paste, and whisk to incorporate.

Transfer the mixture to the top of the pie, spreading it out to the edges, making sure the grapefruit filling is completely covered. Create swoops and spikes with the back of a spoon. Using a culinary torch, toast the meringue all over the surface. Alternatively, you can also place the pie under the broiler of an oven, but be sure to watch it like a hawk, as it has a tendency to burn quickly. Sprinkle the flaky salt on the meringue, slice the pie and serve. This pie is best eaten the same day the meringue is made.

HOT TIP: The raspberry powder does not add flavor here; it serves as a natural way to turn the curd filling a beautiful pale pink, though this is completely optional. To make freeze-dried raspberry powder, simply grind about ¼ cup (15 g) of freeze-dried raspberries in a food processor or crush them in a resealable plastic bag with a rolling pin. Use a mesh strainer to strain out the seeds.

HONEY TAHINI MOUSSE TART

Tahini is having a moment. Much like peanut or other nut butters, its versatility transcends both sweet and savory categories. While each nut and seed butter has its place, tahini seems to have a more refined quality. It's toasty, creamy, complex, slightly bitter and ultrarich. This tart is creamy and light all at once, with a light floral honey flavor weaved throughout that pairs so beautifully with the tahini; the yogurt adds an unexpected and pleasant tanginess. Enjoy a chilled slice of this on a warm summer afternoon.

YIELD
Makes 1 (12-inch [30-cm]) tart

INGREDIENTS
Crust
- ¼ cup + 1 tbsp (50 g) white sesame seeds, divided
- 6 tbsp (84 g) unsalted butter
- ¼ cup (60 ml) honey
- 8 oz (227 g) graham crackers (1½ sleeves)
- Pinch of sea salt

Filling
- 1¼ cups (300 ml) tahini
- 1½ cups (360 ml) thick full-fat Greek yogurt
- ¾ cup (180 ml) honey
- 2 tsp (10 ml) vanilla bean paste
- ¼ tsp sea salt
- 1 cup (240 ml) heavy whipping cream, whipped to stiff peaks

For Serving
- 1 tbsp (10 g) bee pollen, for serving (see tip)

DIRECTIONS
For the crust, preheat the oven to 350°F (177°C). In a skillet over medium-low heat, toast the sesame seeds, tossing occasionally so they don't burn, until they're golden brown and fragrant, 3 to 5 minutes. Transfer the seeds to a small bowl and set them aside to cool.

In a small saucepan over medium-low heat, melt the butter. Once it's melted, remove the pan from the heat, and stir in the honey.

In a food processor, pulse the graham crackers until they resemble fine breadcrumbs. Transfer the crumbs to a large bowl, then add the butter and honey mixture, ¼ cup (40 g) of the toasted sesame seeds and the salt. Mix until the ingredients are well combined and the mixture is clumpy.

Transfer the mixture to a 12-inch (30-cm) fluted tart pan with a removable bottom. Press the mixture into the bottom and sides evenly, using a glass or round measuring cup to press the crumbs evenly around all the sides and pressing down on the bottom to ensure the crust is firmly pressed into the whole tart pan. Bake the crust for 15 to 20 minutes, until it's golden brown and smells toasty. If the bottom puffs up a bit during baking, just gently press it back down again with the bottom of a glass or measuring cup once it's finished baking. Cool the crust completely before filling it, about 30 minutes.

For the filling, in a large bowl, whisk together the tahini, yogurt, honey, vanilla bean paste and salt until smooth. Gently fold in the whipped cream, and mix until the mixture is homogenous. Transfer the filling to the baked crust, and smooth the top with an offset spatula or the back of a spoon. Refrigerate the tart for at least 4 hours and up to overnight before serving it.

To serve, sprinkle the tart with the remaining tablespoon (10 g) of toasted sesame seeds and the bee pollen.

HOT TIP: Bee pollen can usually be found at health food stores, often in the bulk section. It tastes like little pearls of honey. If you have trouble finding it, you can simply omit it.

FROZEN MINTY MALTED GRASSHOPPER TART

Inspired by the grasshopper frappes I used to order in college during finals week, this tart is like a milkshake and chocolate-covered malted milk ball all rolled into one. The filling starts with a luscious and creamy no-churn ice cream base, with the cooling and refreshing flavor of fresh mint woven throughout. The sweet, minty ice cream sits atop a layer of silky, fudgy and rich ganache, which has just the right amount of nutty malted milk. The sweet fillings are tempered by the perfectly crispy, slightly salty dark cocoa crust. This tart is simple to put together and makes a gorgeous dessert to present at a summer dinner party, birthday celebration or anytime a minty, chocolaty craving strikes.

YIELD
Makes 1 (12-inch [30-cm]) tart

INGREDIENTS
Filling
- ½ cup (25 g) packed fresh mint, washed and dried well and finely chopped
- 2 cups (480 ml) heavy whipping cream
- 1 (14-oz [396-g]) can sweetened condensed milk
- 1 drop natural green food coloring, or 1 drop yellow and 1 drop blue, optional, for color

Crust
- 1¼ cups (156 g) all-purpose flour
- ⅓ cup (24 g) high-quality cocoa powder
- ¼ cup (33 g) malted milk powder, such as Horlick's or Carnation
- ⅓ cup (64 g) granulated sugar
- ½ tsp sea salt
- 10 tbsp (143 g) unsalted butter, melted and cooled

Ganache
- 6 oz (170 g) dark chocolate, roughly chopped
- Pinch of sea salt
- ½ cup (120 ml) heavy whipping cream
- ⅓ cup (33 g) malted milk powder

For Serving
- Cacao nibs, for garnish

DIRECTIONS

For the filling, in a medium bowl, combine the mint and heavy cream. Cover the bowl and refrigerate the mixture for 8 to 12 hours. Try not to steep over the 12-hour mark, as the mint can become bitter.

For the crust, preheat the oven to 350°F (177°C). In a bowl, sift the flour, cocoa powder and malted milk powder. Add the sugar and salt and whisk to combine. Add the butter and stir the mixture well to combine. Transfer the dough to a 12-inch (30-cm) tart pan with a removable bottom. Using your hands, press the mixture into the bottom and sides evenly. I find it's easiest to start with pressing the sides evenly first, then evenly distribute the remaining dough on the bottom. Place the tart on a rimmed baking sheet and bake it for 20 to 25 minutes, until it's crisp. If the bottom puffs up a bit during baking, just gently press it back down again with the bottom of a glass or measuring cup once it's finished baking.

(continued)

FROZEN MINTY MALTED GRASSHOPPER TART (CONTINUED)

Meanwhile, make the ganache. Put the chocolate and salt in a medium bowl. In a small pot over medium heat, heat the cream until it's warm but not boiling, 3 to 5 minutes. Pour the cream over the chocolate, completely covering it, and cover the bowl with plastic wrap. Let the mixture stand for 5 minutes. Remove the plastic wrap, and stir the now-melted chocolate to fully incorporate it with the cream. Add the malted milk powder, and stir again to incorporate. Pour the ganache into the bottom of the cooled tart shell, and spread it in an even layer with an offset spatula. Set the tart aside to set up at room temperature while you make the filling.

Strain the mint from the heavy cream and discard it. In a large bowl, use a hand mixer or a whisk to beat the cream to stiff peaks. Drizzle the sweetened condensed milk over the cream, and use a rubber spatula to gently fold it in until it's fully incorporated, being careful not to deflate the cream. For a light green hue, add the food coloring, if using, and stir the mixture again gently to combine.

Add the filling to the tart shell, spread it into an even layer and make decorative swoops with the back of a spoon. Freeze the tart until it's frozen solid, at least 8 hours or overnight.

To serve, sprinkle the tart with the cacao nibs. Serve the tart frozen.

SPUMONI ICEBOX PIE

Spumoni, not to be confused with its more basic cousin Neapolitan, is traditionally a trio of deep chocolate, rich cherry and nutty pistachio gelati that is truly greater than the sum of its parts. Each flavor is wonderful on its own and even better together. My earliest memory of spumoni ice cream is the little sundae they bring you after a meal at The Old Spaghetti Factory. It also happens to be my dad's favorite flavor, so I grew up eating it on occasion as well. And by eating it, I mean eating mostly only the chocolate stripe and picking around the cherry and pistachio chunks. Here, I've updated the classic gelato into a decadent layered ice cream pie with a rich ganache base and layers of creamy cherry and pistachio ice cream, all nestled in a pistachio shortbread crust. Though it takes a bit of time to prepare, this is perhaps one of the simplest pies in this book, and it has major wow-factor vibes for whomever you serve it to.

YIELD
Makes 1 (9-inch [23-cm]) pie

INGREDIENTS
Crust
· ¾ cup (110 g) unsalted shelled pistachios, divided
· ⅓ cup (64 g) granulated sugar
· 1½ cups (187 g) all-purpose flour
· ½ tsp sea salt
· 10 tbsp (143 g) unsalted butter, melted and cooled

Ganache
· 6 oz (170 g) dark chocolate, roughly chopped
· Pinch of sea salt
· ½ cup (120 ml) heavy whipping cream
· 4 tbsp (56 g) unsalted butter, room temperature

Filling
· 2 cups (480 ml) heavy whipping cream
· 1 (14-oz [396-g]) can sweetened condensed milk
· ¼ cup (75 g) cherry preserves, such as Bonne Maman®
· ⅓ cup (80 g) drained high-quality maraschino cherries, such as Luxardo, halved
· 2½ tsp (13 ml) almond extract, divided
· 1 drop natural green food coloring, or 1 drop yellow and 1 drop blue, optional

DIRECTIONS
For the crust, preheat the oven to 350°F (177°C), and line a rimmed baking sheet with foil. Process the pistachios in the bowl of a food processor, pulsing until they are a finely ground powder, about 1 minute or so. Be careful not to process the pistachios for too long, or they'll start to release their oils and turn into pistachio butter. Set aside ½ cup (74 g) of the ground pistachios. In a bowl, whisk to combine the remaining ¼ cup (36 g) of pistachios with the sugar, flour and salt. Pour in the butter, and stir well to combine it.

Transfer the dough to a 9-inch (23-cm) springform pan with a removable bottom. Press the mixture into the bottom and all the way up the sides evenly. Place the pan on the prepared baking sheet, and bake the crust for 20 to 25 minutes, until golden brown. If the bottom puffs up a bit during baking, just gently press it back down again with the bottom of a glass or measuring cup once it's finished baking. Cool the crust completely before filling it.

(continued)

SPUMONI ICEBOX PIE (CONTINUED)

To make the ganache, put the chocolate and salt in a bowl. In a small pot over medium heat, heat the cream until it's warm but not boiling, 3 to 5 minutes. Pour the cream over the chocolate, completely covering it, cover the bowl with plastic wrap and let it stand for 5 minutes. Remove the plastic wrap, and stir the now-melted chocolate to fully incorporate it with the cream. Add the butter, a few cubes at a time, stirring each time to fully incorporate it. If you find the butter isn't quite melting into the ganache, heat the bowl in a microwave in 5- to 10-second increments, then give it another stir. Pour the ganache into the bottom of the cooled pie shell, and spread it in an even layer with the back of a spoon. Refrigerate the pie to set the ganache, 20 to 30 minutes.

Make the filling's cherry ice cream layer. Beat the heavy cream to stiff peaks, 2 to 4 minutes, in the bowl of a stand mixer or using a large bowl and a hand mixer. Drizzle in the sweetened condensed milk, and use a rubber spatula to gently fold it in until fully incorporated, being careful not to deflate the cream. Transfer half of the mixture to another bowl, and refrigerate it for the pistachio layer. To the remaining mixture, add the cherry preserves, cherries and ½ teaspoon of the almond extract; stir gently to incorporate the ingredients. Pour the mixture over the ganache, smooth it into an even layer and freeze it until it's very firm, about 1 to 2 hours.

When you're ready to add the pistachio layer to the pie, pull the reserved cream and condensed milk mixture from the fridge. Add the remaining 2 teaspoons (10 ml) of almond extract, reserved ½ cup (74 g) of ground pistachios and food coloring, if using, and fold gently to combine. Pour the mixture over the cherry layer, smooth it into an even layer, then use the back of a spoon to make decorative swoops or a swirl on the top. Freeze the pie until it's completely solid, at least 4 hours and up to overnight. To serve, release and remove the springform pan and slice the pie.

MOCHA COCONUT CREAM PIE

Toasty tropical coconut, bitter and caramelly sweet espresso and rich dark chocolate come together to create an epic and over-the-top coconut cream pie like you've never had before. It's a chocolate and coffee lover's dream! I even almost got detention for this flavor combination. Senior year of high school, I racked up too many tardies to first period—be cool, it was just AP studio art—for making a pitstop to Starbucks each morning to grab a mocha coconut Frappuccino. Worth it. The mocha coconut custard in this pie is so velvety and rich it's almost fudgy, and it's perfectly balanced with the cloud of whipped cream, which is gratuitously showered in toasted coconut chips and curls of dark chocolate. It's a true revelatory experience, even worth getting detention for.

YIELD
Makes 1 (9-inch [23-cm]) pie

INGREDIENTS
Crust
· ½ recipe All-Purpose Dough (page 22), patted into a disc

Filling
· ½ cup (100 g) granulated sugar
· ¼ cup (35 g) cornstarch
· 2 tbsp (10 g) instant espresso powder
· ½ tsp sea salt
· 2 cups (480 ml) whole milk
· 4 large egg yolks
· 1 tsp coconut extract
· 4 oz (113 g) 60–70% cacao dark chocolate, finely chopped
· 4 tbsp (56 g) unsalted butter, room temperature, cut into small pieces

For Serving
· 1 cup (129 g) Honey Whipped Cream (page 175)
· ½ cup (27 g) unsweetened coconut chips, toasted
· Shaved dark chocolate

DIRECTIONS

For the crust, on a well-floured surface, roll the dough out to a ¼-inch (6-mm) thick round about 12 inches (30 cm) in diameter. Transfer the dough to a 9-inch (23-cm) pie pan and position it so that it's centered with about an inch (2.5 cm) of dough hanging over the sides. Tuck the excess dough underneath itself. Crimp the edges by pinching the dough between your thumb and index finger, and press the dough between those fingers with your other thumb, pressing down slightly to adhere the edge of dough to the pan. Repeat around the whole edge. Prick the bottom of the crust all over with a fork, and freeze it for 30 minutes.

Meanwhile, preheat the oven to 425°F (218°C), and line a rimmed baking sheet with parchment paper or foil.

To blind-bake the crust, cut a piece of parchment paper large enough to fit inside the pie shell and up the sides with a few extra inches of overhang. Crumple up the parchment a few times to soften it. Smooth it out and fit it inside the pie shell. Fill up to the top of the pie with pie weights, dried beans or rice. Bake the crust on the prepared baking sheet for 20 minutes, until the crust is just set. Remove the weights by lifting out the whole piece of parchment. Reduce the temperature of the oven to 350°F (177°C), and bake the crust for 30 to 35 minutes, or until the crust is a deep golden brown and is crisp. Wrap the crimped edges lightly in foil, if they're getting too brown before the bottom has crisped properly. Cool the crust completely before filling it.

(continued)

MOCHA COCONUT CREAM PIE (CONTINUED)

To make the filling, combine the sugar, cornstarch, espresso powder and salt in a heavy-bottomed saucepan; whisk to combine. Add the milk and egg yolks, and whisk again to combine. Cook over medium heat, whisking constantly, for 5 to 7 minutes, or until the mixture is thick and glossy. It should be the consistency of pudding.

Pour the mixture through a fine-mesh strainer set over a large bowl, and press the mixture through gently with a rubber spatula to strain out any clumps. Whisk in the coconut extract, then add the chocolate and continue whisking until it's completely melted and incorporated. Add the butter, a few pieces at a time, and whisk again until the butter is fully incorporated. Pour the filling into the cooled pie shell, and smooth it into an even layer. Place a piece of plastic wrap directly on top of the filling to prevent a film from forming. Refrigerate the pie until the filling is set, at least 4 hours.

To serve, top the pie with the Honey Whipped Cream and sprinkle it with the coconut chips and chocolate shavings.

ROSEMARY DARK CHOCOLATE GANACHE TART

Earthy rosemary is a surprisingly well-suited companion for dark chocolate, and the flavor comes through beautifully in this silky, rich ganache. The combination always reminds me of the holidays and makes a simple, yet elegant, dessert to serve at a holiday party with some coffee. I will caution you that this is a very rich tart, not unlike a candy bar, and just a small sliver is all you need.

YIELD
Makes 1 (14 x 4–inch [36 x 10–cm]) tart

INGREDIENTS
· ½ recipe All-Purpose Dough (page 22), herb variation with rosemary, patted into a rectangle

· ½ cup (120 ml) heavy whipping cream

· 3 sprigs (10 g) fresh rosemary

· 10 oz (283 g) dark chocolate bars, roughly chopped (see tip)

· Pinch of sea salt

· 3 tbsp (42 g) unsalted butter, room temperature, cut into small pieces

· Flaky salt, for serving

HOT TIP: I recommend using high-quality chocolate bars rather than chips here, as chocolate chips contain stabilizers that can affect the final result of the ganache.

THINK SCRAPPY! Have some leftover dough scraps? Put them to good use with a recipe from the Waste Not, Want Not chapter (page 181).

DIRECTIONS
Preheat the oven to 375°F (190°C), and line a rimmed baking sheet with parchment paper or foil.

On a well-floured surface, roll the dough out into a ¼-inch (6-mm) thick rectangle, then transfer it to a 14 x 4–inch (36 x 10–cm) tart pan with a removable bottom. Drape the dough down the side of the pan, so as to not stretch out the dough. Using your thumb, trim away the excess dough by gently pressing the dough against the scalloped edge of the pan. Prick all over the bottom and sides of the dough gently with the tines of a fork. Freeze the tart for about 30 minutes, until very firm.

Place the tart shell on the prepared baking sheet. Cut a piece of parchment paper large enough to fit inside the pie shell and up the sides, with a few extra inches of overhang. Crumple up the parchment a few times to soften it. Smooth it out and fit it inside the tart shell. Fill up to the top of the tart with pie weights, dried beans or rice. Bake the tart for 15 to 20 minutes, until the dough is set. Remove the weights and the parchment, and bake the shell for 10 to 15 minutes, until it's golden brown and the bottom is crisp. Set aside the shell to cool completely before filling it.

Meanwhile, in a small saucepan, bring the cream and rosemary sprigs to a simmer over medium heat. Remove the pan from the heat, cover it and let the mixture steep for 30 minutes.

Put the chocolate and sea salt in a medium bowl, and set it aside.

After the steeping time, remove the rosemary from the cream and heat it until it's warm but not boiling, 3 to 5 minutes. Pour it over the chocolate, and cover the bowl with plastic wrap. Let it stand for 5 minutes. Remove the plastic wrap and stir the melted chocolate and cream to combine. Add the butter, a few cubes at a time, and stir to combine it. Pour the filling into the cooled tart shell, and refrigerate until it is set, about 1 hour.

To serve, sprinkle the tart with the flaky salt.

DIRTY CHAI CHESS PIE

The dirty chai is a chai latte spiked with a shot of espresso. This may sound like the flavors would clash, but the combination of sweet and earthy, warming spices and deep, almost caramelly espresso somehow works. Blending these flavors into the chess pie, a traditional custard pie of the South, results in a spicy, velvety, creamy filling, which rests in a shatteringly crisp crust, for the perfect textural contrast.

YIELD
Makes 1 (9-inch [23-cm]) pie

INGREDIENTS
· ½ recipe All-Purpose Dough (page 22), patted into a disc
· 3 tbsp (24 g) all-purpose flour
· 1 tbsp (5 g) instant espresso powder
· 2 tsp (3 g) ground cinnamon
· 1½ tsp (5 g) ground ginger
· ¾ tsp ground cardamom
· ½ tsp freshly ground black pepper
· ⅛ tsp freshly grated nutmeg
· ⅛ tsp ground cloves
· 1¼ tsp (6 g) sea salt
· 3 large eggs, room temperature
· ¼ cup (60 ml) heavy whipping cream, room temperature
· 1 cup (200 g) granulated sugar
· ¼ cup (65 g) packed light brown sugar
· 2 tsp (10 ml) distilled white vinegar
· 2 tsp (10 g) vanilla bean paste
· ½ cup (112 ml) unsalted butter, melted and cooled
· Powdered sugar, for serving

VARIATION: Try this recipe with Buttermilk Dough (page 24).

DIRECTIONS
Preheat the oven to 375°F (190°C), and line a rimmed baking sheet with parchment paper or foil.

On a well-floured surface, roll the dough out to a ¼- to ⅛-inch (6- to 3-mm) thick round about 12 inches (30 cm) in diameter. Transfer the dough to a 9-inch (23-cm) pie pan, and position it so that it's centered with about an inch (2.5 cm) of dough hanging over the sides. Tuck the excess dough underneath itself. Crimp the edges however you'd like using one of the crimping methods (pages 15–16). Prick the bottom all over with a fork, and freeze the crust for 30 minutes.

To blind-bake the crust, cut a piece of parchment paper large enough to fit inside the pie shell and up the sides with a few extra inches of overhang. Crumple up the parchment a few times to soften it. Smooth it out and fit it inside the pie shell. Fill up to the top of the pie with pie weights, dried beans or rice. Bake the crust on the prepared baking sheet for 20 minutes, until the crust is just set. Then, remove the weights by lifting out the whole piece of parchment. Bake the crust for 5 minutes, or until it just goes from shiny to matte. Remove the crust from the oven, and reduce its temperature to 350°F (177°C).

Meanwhile, make the filling. In a small bowl, whisk together the flour, espresso powder, cinnamon, ginger, cardamom, pepper, nutmeg, cloves and salt.

In a large bowl, combine the eggs, cream, granulated and brown sugars, vinegar and vanilla bean paste; whisk until the mixture is smooth. Drizzle in the butter and whisk to incorporate. Add the flour mixture, and whisk again until smooth. Pour the filling into the pie shell and carefully place the pie in the oven. Bake the pie for 50 to 55 minutes, until the filling is set and the center is just a touch wobbly. Cool the pie completely before serving it, at least 2 hours.

To serve, generously dust the surface with the powdered sugar, using a stencil—cookie cutters and paper lace doilies work great—if desired to create a design.

SPICED CRANBERRY CURD TART

This festive little tart has become a favorite around the holidays. The bright and tart cranberry curd is tempered with cozy and warming spices and a gingerbread-like crust that's unmistakably wintery. It's deceptively simple to put the tart together, and it may be made a day in advance and stored in the fridge. The day of, simply top it with the whipped cream and toppings, and it's ready for any holiday soiree you have in store.

YIELD
Makes 1 (12-inch [30-cm]) tart

INGREDIENTS
Crust
- 6 tbsp (84 g) unsalted butter
- 2 tbsp (30 ml) honey
- 2 tbsp (30 ml) molasses
- 8 oz (227 g) graham crackers, 1½ sleeves
- 1 tsp ground cinnamon
- 2 tsp (6 g) ground ginger
- Pinch of sea salt

Filling
- 12 oz fresh cranberries, washed, or thawed frozen cranberries
- ½ cup (120 ml) water
- ¼ cup (60 ml) freshly squeezed orange juice
- 2 cinnamon sticks
- 3 cardamom pods, lightly crushed
- 2 cloves
- 1-inch (2.5-cm) chunk fresh ginger, cut into thin coins

- ¾ cup (150 g) granulated sugar
- 4 large egg yolks
- 4 tbsp (56 g) butter, room temperature, cut into small pieces
- Zest of 1 orange, finely grated

For Serving
- Honey Whipped Cream (page 175)
- 1 tbsp (5 g) finely chopped crystallized ginger
- A few fresh cranberries, thinly sliced into coins

DIRECTIONS
For the crust, preheat the oven to 350°F (177°C). In a small saucepan over medium-low heat, melt the butter. Once it's melted, remove the pan from the heat, and stir in the honey and molasses. Set aside the pan.

In a food processor, pulse the graham crackers until the mixture resembles fine breadcrumbs. Transfer the crumbs to a large bowl, and add the butter and honey-molasses mixture, cinnamon, ginger and salt. Mix until the ingredients are well combined and the mixture is clumpy. Transfer the mixture to a 12-inch (30-cm) fluted tart pan with a removable bottom. Press the mixture into the bottom and sides evenly, using a glass or round measuring cup to press the crumbs evenly around all the sides and pressing down on the bottom to ensure the crust is firmly pressed into the whole tart pan. Bake the crust for 12 to 15 minutes, until it's golden brown and set. If the bottom puffs up a bit during baking, just gently press it back down again with the bottom of a glass or measuring cup, once it's finished baking.

(continued)

SPICED CRANBERRY CURD TART (CONTINUED)

Meanwhile, make the filling. In a saucepan over medium heat, bring the cranberries, water, orange juice, cinnamon, cardamom, cloves and ginger to a simmer. Turn the heat down to low, and cook the mixture until the cranberries pop and have broken down, about 12 to 15 minutes.

While the cranberry mixture cooks, combine the sugar and egg yolks in a bowl, whisk them until they are pale in color, about 2 minutes, then set aside.

Pour the cranberry mixture into a fine-mesh strainer set over a bowl, pressing the pulp gently with a spoon to get as much puree out as possible. Be sure to scrape the underside of the strainer as well to get all the puree. Discard the pulp and spices and pour the strained puree back into the saucepan. Add the egg mixture and cook over medium heat, whisking constantly, until the consistency thickens enough to coat the back of a spoon, 5 to 7 minutes. Remove the pan from the heat; stir in the butter and orange zest. Pour the filling into the crust, and bake the tart until the curd is firm, with just a slight wobble in the center, 12 to 15 minutes. Cool completely at room temperature, then refrigerate the tart until the filling is completely set, at least 2 hours.

To serve, dollop the Honey Whipped Cream on top and spread it into an even layer, making decorative swoops with the back of a spoon. Sprinkle the cream with the ginger and cranberry slices.

MAPLE MERINGUE SWEET POTATO PIE

To some, a sweet potato pie is nothing more than an alt pumpkin pie, but it's really its own thing and deserves its own space in the pie-sphere. The rich and velvety filling has a modest amount of spice, but the real star is the tender sweet potatoes that lend themselves so well to a dessert thanks to their natural sugars. I've added some sour cream for richness and to add some tang. The hazelnut crust and fluffy meringue sweetened with pure maple syrup is a flavor combination so good, you'll wonder why you haven't always been making this pie.

YIELD
Makes 1 (9-inch [23-cm]) pie

INGREDIENTS
Crust
- ½ recipe Any-Nut Dough (page 27), using hazelnuts, patted into a disc

Filling
- 1½ lbs (681 g) sweet potatoes, about 2 large, peeled and cut into 1-inch (2.5-cm) cubes
- 2 large eggs, room temperature
- ½ cup (100 g) granulated sugar
- ¾ cup (180 ml) full-fat sour cream
- 4 tbsp (56 g) butter, melted and cooled
- 1 tsp vanilla bean paste
- 1½ tsp (5 g) ground cinnamon
- ¼ tsp ground nutmeg
- ½ tsp sea salt

Meringue
- 3 large egg whites, room temperature
- ¼ tsp cream of tartar
- 1 cup (240 ml) pure maple syrup

DIRECTIONS
For the crust, preheat the oven to 425°F (218°C), and line a rimmed baking sheet with parchment paper or foil.

On a well-floured surface, roll the dough out to a ¼- to ⅛-inch (6- to 3-mm) thick round about 12 inches (30 cm) in diameter. Transfer the dough to a 9-inch (23-cm) pie pan and position it so that it's centered with about an inch (2.5 cm) of dough hanging over the sides. Tuck the excess dough underneath itself. Crimp the edges however you'd like using one of the crimping methods (pages 15–16). Freeze the crust for 30 minutes.

Place the pie on the prepared baking sheet. Cut a piece of parchment paper large enough to fit inside the pie shell and up the sides, with a few extra inches of overhang. Crumple up the parchment a few times to soften it. Smooth it out and fit it inside the pie shell. Fill up to the top of the pie with pie weights, dried beans or rice. Bake the crust for 20 minutes, until dough is set and starting to get a little color on the edges. Remove the weights and parchment, and bake the shell for 10 minutes or so, until the crust is just light golden but still quite blonde. Reduce the oven temperature to 350°F (177°C).

(continued)

MAPLE MERINGUE SWEET POTATO PIE (CONTINUED)

For the filling, bring a large pot of water to a boil. Add the sweet potatoes, and boil them until they are tender when poked with a fork, 8 to 10 minutes. Drain the sweet potatoes. In the bowl of a food processor, process the sweet potatoes until smooth, 2 to 3 minutes. Transfer the sweet potato puree to a large bowl. Add the eggs, sugar, sour cream, butter, vanilla bean paste, cinnamon, nutmeg and salt, and whisk until everything is well incorporated.

Pour the filling into the crust and smooth it into an even layer. Bake the pie for 50 to 55 minutes, until the filling is set with just a slight wobble in the center when you jiggle the pan. Cool the pie completely, at least 2 hours.

For the meringue, beat the egg whites and cream of tartar in the bowl of a stand mixer fitted with the whisk attachment until they are frothy, about a minute or so.

In a medium heavy-bottomed saucepan, cook the maple syrup over medium heat, swirling occasionally, until it reaches 240°F (116°C). Remove the syrup from the heat. With the mixer running on medium-low speed, slowly stream the maple syrup into the egg whites. Once it's all incorporated, turn the mixer up to high and beat the mixture until stiff peaks form. Transfer the meringue to the top of the pie, use the back of a spoon to smooth out the meringue, then make some swoops and peaks. Or, fill a piping bag fitted with a star tip with the meringue and pipe rosettes all over the top. Using a culinary torch, toast the meringue all over the surface. Alternatively, you can place the pie under the broiler of an oven, but be sure to watch it like a hawk, as it has a tendency to burn quickly. Serve the pie immediately.

GOOEY OATMEAL COOKIE PIE

Think of this pie as a cross between a chewy molasses cookie and a gooey, brown sugar oatmeal cookie. A rich, oat and brown sugar–laden custard is baked to perfection in a crispy crust with hints of warming spices. A scoop of vanilla ice cream is a must.

YIELD

Makes 1 (9-inch [23-cm]) pie

INGREDIENTS

· ½ recipe All-Purpose Dough (page 22), patted into a disc
· 1½ cups (150 g) old-fashioned rolled oats
· 3 large eggs, room temperature
· 1 cup (260 g) light brown sugar
· 1 tbsp (15 ml) molasses
· 6 tbsp (84 g) butter, melted and cooled
· ⅓ cup (80 ml) heavy whipping cream
· 1 tbsp (15 ml) vanilla bean paste
· 2 tbsp (18 g) cornstarch
· 2 tsp (3 g) ground cinnamon
· ½ tsp ground nutmeg
· 1 tsp sea salt
· Vanilla ice cream, for serving

DIRECTIONS

Preheat the oven to 375°F (190°C), and line a rimmed baking sheet with foil.

On a well-floured surface, roll the dough out to a ¼-inch (6-mm) thick round about 12 inches (30 cm) in diameter. Transfer the dough to a 9-inch (23-cm) pie pan, and position it so that it's centered with about an inch (2.5 cm) of dough hanging over the sides. Tuck the excess dough underneath itself. Crimp the edges however you'd like using one of the crimping methods (pages 15–16). Freeze the crust for 30 minutes.

Spread the oats out on a rimmed baking sheet, and bake them for 13 to 15 minutes, until they smell toasty and reach a light golden color. Remove the oats from the oven, and set them aside to cool for a few minutes.

In a large bowl, whisk together the eggs, brown sugar, molasses, butter, cream, vanilla bean paste, cornstarch, cinnamon, nutmeg and salt. Add the toasted oats, and stir to combine the ingredients. Pour the filling into the crust. Bake the pie on the prepared baking sheet for 55 to 60 minutes, until the top is set but the center has the slightest wobble when you shake the pan. If the crust is getting too dark before the filling is cooked through, lightly wrap it in foil. Cool the pie completely before slicing it, at least 2 hours. Serve the slices with a scoop of vanilla ice cream.

VARIATION: Try this recipe with Brown Butter Dough (page 23).

SALTED CARAMEL PUMPKIN TART

Wanna know how to make an ultrapumpkin pie even more decadent? Swirl a little—or a lot—of buttery salted clementine caramel sauce into it. The perfectly spiced earthy filling is the ideal foundation for the sticky, sweet caramel sauce and bakes up into a beautiful swirl pattern. This tart is wonderful the day it's made, but even better the next day, making it ideal for make-ahead prep for holiday get-togethers.

YIELD
Makes 1 (12-inch [30 cm]) tart

INGREDIENTS

Crust
· ½ recipe Brown Butter Dough (page 23), patted into a disc

Filling
· 1 (15-oz [425-g]) can pumpkin puree
· ½ cup (130 g) brown sugar
· ¼ cup (50 g) granulated sugar
· 2 large eggs, room temperature
· ½ cup (120 ml) heavy whipping cream
· 1 tsp vanilla bean paste
· 2 tsp (5 g) pumpkin pie spice
· ½ tsp sea salt
· ½ cup (120 ml) Salted Clementine Caramel Sauce (page 179)

For Serving
· Honey Whipped Cream (page 175) or ice cream

HOT TIP: To make prep a bit easier the day of, make the Salted Clementine Caramel Sauce a day in advance. It can be stored on the counter at room temperature.

DIRECTIONS

For the crust, preheat the oven to 375°F (190°C), and line a rimmed baking sheet with parchment paper or foil. On a well-floured surface, roll the dough out into a ⅛-inch (3-mm) thick round, and transfer it to a 12-inch (30-cm) round tart pan with a removable bottom. Drape the dough down the side of the pan so as to not stretch out the dough. Using your thumb, trim away the excess dough by gently pressing the dough against the scalloped edge of the pan. Prick all over the bottom of the crust gently with the tines of a fork. Freeze the shell for about 30 minutes, until very firm.

Place the tart shell on the prepared baking sheet. Cut a piece of parchment paper large enough to fit inside the pie shell and up the sides, with a few extra inches of overhang. Crumple up the parchment a few times to soften it. Smooth it out and fit it inside the pie shell. Fill up to the top of the pie with pie weights, dried beans or rice. Bake the shell for 20 minutes, until the dough is set and starting to get a little color on the edges. Remove the weights and parchment, and bake the shell for 10 minutes or so, until the crust is just light golden but still quite blonde. Reduce the oven temperature to 350°F (177°C).

Meanwhile, make the filling. In a large bowl, whisk together the pumpkin, brown and granulated sugars, eggs, cream, vanilla bean paste, pumpkin pie spice and salt until the ingredients are combined. Pour the pumpkin filling into the tart shell, and jiggle the tart gently to smooth out the surface.

If the caramel sauce is especially thick, heat it in a glass heatproof measuring cup or bowl in the microwave in 10-second increments, until the consistency is about that of honey: still thick but pourable. Using a spoon, add spoonfuls of the caramel all over the surface of the tart. Using a wooden skewer or the tip of a knife, swirl the caramel with the pumpkin filling to create a marbled effect. Bake the tart for 35 to 40 minutes, until the filling is just set but wiggles just a bit in the center when you jiggle the pan. Cool the tart completely before slicing and serving it. Garnish the tart slices with a dollop of the Honey Whipped Cream or ice cream.

PAPA'S GOLDEN PECAN PIE

My grandpa Dale adored a pecan pie. He had an unrelenting sweet tooth and, while he was a diehard fan of corn syrup—he used to slather it on his toast with peanut butter—I'm partial to the caramelized flavor of golden syrup, a by-product of cane sugar. It adds a delicious depth to the pie that I think he would approve of. And, although he was not a big drinker despite working as a foreman at the Olympia Brewery for over 30 years, I think he would have appreciated the hint of bourbon, too, which helps to cut the richness and adds warmth. The slight bitter edge from the buckwheat crust serves to bring a bit of balance with the rich and sweet filling. He passed away a few years ago, and I miss him more than my words can express. Pop, this one's for you.

YIELD
Makes 1 (9-inch [23-cm]) pie

INGREDIENTS
Crust
· ½ recipe Buckwheat Dough (page 29), patted into a disc

Filling
· 3 large eggs, room temperature
· ¾ cup (195 g) dark brown sugar
· 1 cup (240 ml) golden syrup, such as Lyle's
· 6 tbsp (84 g) butter, melted and cooled
· 2 tbsp (30 ml) bourbon
· 1 tbsp (15 ml) vanilla bean paste
· 1 tsp sea salt
· 2 cups (244 g) toasted pecan halves, roughly chopped

For Serving
· Honey Whipped Cream (page 175) or ice cream

DIRECTIONS

For the crust, on a well-floured surface, roll the dough out to a ¼- to ⅛-inch (6- to 3-mm) thick round about 12 inches (30 cm) in diameter. Transfer the dough to a 9-inch (23-cm) pie pan and position it so that it's centered with about an inch (2.5 cm) of dough hanging over the sides. Tuck the excess dough underneath itself. Crimp the edges however you'd like using one of the crimping methods (pages 15–16). Freeze the crust for 30 minutes.

Preheat the oven to 350°F (177°C), and line a rimmed baking sheet with foil.

Meanwhile, for the filling, in a medium bowl whisk the eggs, brown sugar, golden syrup, butter, bourbon, vanilla bean paste and salt to combine the ingredients. Fold in the pecans. Pour the filling into the crust.

Bake the pie on the prepared baking sheet for 65 to 75 minutes, until the top is set but the center has the slightest wobble when you shake the pan. If the crust is getting too dark before the filling is cooked through, lightly wrap it in foil. Cool the pie completely before slicing it, at least 2 hours.

Serve the pie with the Honey Whipped Cream or vanilla ice cream.

THE SAVORY SIDE

When most of us think of pie, I bet a savory one isn't the first thought that comes to mind. If you fall into this camp, there's a whole world of savory pie just waiting to be tapped. Think of them as an opportunity to get a meal on the table all in one go, but with the most flavor payoff possible. Many of the recipes in this chapter are familiar flavors reborn in pie form. These recipes are a chance to experience and share some of your favorite dishes in a completely new and unexpected way. It's even more fun if your guests aren't expecting a pie for dinner. Ask your friends if they like French onion soup and then watch their faces light up when you bring a Caramelized Onion and Gruyère Galette (page 135) to the table. Or my favorite, a cozy artichoke dip in the form of a Kale and Artichoke Galette (page 122), with its tangy, vinegary bite and creamy texture full of sharp Parmigiano.

There are plenty of updated, familiar classics, too, like Deep-Dish Broccoli Cheddar Chicken Pot Pie (page 115), a family treasure of tender, juicy chicken and perfectly crisp-tender vegetables smothered in cheddar sauce and baked to golden perfection in an herb-laden crust. The rule with this pie in our house is: if you're going to the trouble of making one, you have to make two. The second may be squirreled away for another meal or gifted to a lucky neighbor or friend. Classic quiche and the Middle Eastern favorite shakshuka converge in Smoky Shakshuka Quiche (page 107), an opportunity to enjoy all the spicy and flavorful stewed tomato and peppers in a convenient, all-in-one egg and pastry package. Serve it for brunch, lunch or dinner.

With the seasons in mind, there's plenty of opportunity to make use of your garden's abundance as well, should you be lucky enough to have one. I can't think of a better way to enjoy fresh tomatoes than in the Fresh Corn and Heirloom Tomato Pie with Cheddar and Chives (page 111).

I hope you find some new favorites in this chapter, and have fun exploring all that savory pies have to offer.

TANGY, SPICY CARROT TARTE TATIN

This is a very unexpectedly delicious pie, indeed. Not only is layering up the carrots in a sort of jigsaw intensely satisfying, but the flavors are some of my favorites, each one in perfect harmony with one another. The sweetness from the carrots and honey is tempered by the spicy pepper flakes, and the lime and sumac combine for a mouth-puckering tart finish that will make you keep going back for another bite. The blanket of crisp, buttery walnut crust holds it all together. Serve this as a light lunch with a salad or an anytime snack making use of an abundance of spring carrots.

YIELD
Makes 1 (9-inch [23-cm]) tarte Tatin

INGREDIENTS

- 1 lb (454 g) carrots, peeled or scrubbed, root end removed and halved lengthwise
- 1 tbsp (15 ml) olive oil
- ½ tsp sea salt
- ¼ tsp freshly ground black pepper
- 1½ tsp (3 g) Aleppo pepper flakes or crushed red pepper, divided
- 2 tsp (7 g) sumac, plus more for sprinkling on top
- Zest of 2 limes, finely grated
- 2 tbsp (30 ml) freshly squeezed lime juice
- 3 tbsp (45 ml) honey
- ½ recipe Any-Nut Dough (page 27), using walnuts, patted into a disc
- Citrusy Whipped Yogurt (page 176), for serving
- Roughly chopped fresh tender herbs, such as cilantro, chives, mint or dill, for serving

DIRECTIONS

Preheat the oven to 400°F (204°C). In a large bowl, toss the carrots to coat them with the olive oil, salt, black pepper, ½ teaspoon of the Aleppo pepper flakes and sumac. Spread the carrots out on a rimmed baking sheet in a single layer, cut side down. Roast the carrots for 25 to 30 minutes, until they are tender and just starting to brown.

Meanwhile, combine the lime zest and juice, honey and remaining teaspoon of the Aleppo pepper in a small saucepan. Heat the mixture over medium heat until the honey has thinned out, then cook it until the mixture is bubbling and has thickened slightly, 5 to 7 minutes, swirling occasionally to ensure the honey doesn't burn. Shut off the heat, and pour the mixture into the bottom of a 9-inch (23-cm) pie pan, swirling the pan to evenly coat the bottom.

Arrange the carrots in a single layer, cut side down, over the top of the mixture, so they are nestled in closely, alternating the thick and thin ends so the carrots are nestled up against one another. Arrange any remaining carrots on top in another layer.

Line a rimmed baking sheet with foil.

Roll out the dough to a ¼-inch (6-mm) thick disc, about ½ inch (1.3 cm) larger in diameter than the pie plate. Drape the crust over the filling evenly, folding the excess over onto itself. Prick the surface all over with a fork to create some vent holes for steam to escape. Bake the pie on the prepared baking sheet for 15 minutes, then reduce the heat to 375°F (190°C). Bake the pie for 20 to 25 minutes, until the crust is deep golden brown and crisp.

Let the pie cool just a minute or two. Then, while wearing oven mitts, place a large plate over the pie and carefully invert the pie so that it ends up bottom side up on the plate. Sprinkle the pie with sumac, and serve it with a dollop of the Citrusy Whipped Yogurt and fresh herbs. The carrot tarte Tatin is best served the day it is made.

VARIATION: Try this recipe with Rye Dough (page 26).

ASPARAGUS TART WITH HAZELNUTS, ORANGE AND TARRAGON

It wasn't until my sister, cousin and I took a road trip to San Francisco a few years ago and had the most delicious crisp-tender asparagus on toast with nutty Gruyère at Tartine that I really understood what asparagus could be, rather than the mushy spears of my youth. Here I've taken a classic combination of orange, tarragon and asparagus and reimagined it in a luscious tart. The secret to achieving the perfect asparagus texture in this tart is adding it raw. By the time it bakes with the custard, it will be perfectly al dente. The result is a true celebration of asparagus, the way it was always supposed to be.

YIELD
Makes 1 (12-inch [30-cm]) tart

INGREDIENTS
- ½ recipe Any-Nut Dough (page 27), using hazelnuts, patted into a disc
- 1 cup (240 ml) crème fraîche, room temperature
- 2 large eggs, room temperature
- 2 oz (57 g) Comté cheese, grated (see tip)
- Zest of 1 large orange, finely grated
- 2 tsp (4 g) roughly chopped fresh tarragon
- 1 tsp sea salt
- ½ tsp freshly ground black pepper
- 8 oz (227 g) asparagus, woody ends trimmed and cut into ¼-inch (6-mm) pieces on an extreme diagonal
- 1 tbsp (7 g) toasted hazelnuts, roughly chopped, for serving

DIRECTIONS
Preheat the oven to 375°F (190°C), and line a rimmed baking sheet with parchment paper or foil.

On a well-floured surface, roll the dough out into a ¼-inch (6-mm) thick round, and transfer it to a 12-inch (30-cm) round tart pan with a removable bottom. Drape the dough down the side of the pan so as to not stretch out the dough. Using your thumb, trim away the excess dough by gently pressing the dough against the scalloped edge of the pan. Prick all over the bottom of the dough gently with the tines of a fork. Freeze the tart shell for about 30 minutes, until very firm.

Place the tart shell on the prepared baking sheet. Cut a piece of parchment paper large enough to fit inside the tart shell and up the sides, with a few extra inches of overhang. Crumple up the parchment a few times to soften it. Smooth it out and fit it inside the tart shell. Fill up to the top of the tart with pie weights, dried beans or rice. Bake the shell for 20 to 25 minutes, until the dough is set and starting to get a little color on the edges. Remove the weights and parchment, and bake for 15 to 20 minutes, until the crust is golden brown and the bottom is crisp.

Make the custard while the shell is baking. Whisk the crème fraîche, eggs, Comté, orange zest, tarragon, salt and pepper in a medium bowl. Set it aside.

Reduce the oven temperature to 350°F (177°C). Scatter the asparagus evenly in the bottom of the tart shell, reserving a small handful to sprinkle over the top. Carefully pour the custard over the asparagus, distributing it evenly. Scatter the reserved asparagus all over the top. Bake the tart for 20 to 25 minutes, until the custard is set in the center and is light brown in a few spots. Cool the tart for a few minutes before removing it from the tart pan.

Sprinkle the tart with the hazelnuts, and serve it warm or at room temperature.

HOT TIP: If you can't find Comté cheese, Gruyère is a great substitute.

SMOKY SHAKSHUKA QUICHE

Shakshuka, a spicy North African tomato stew with poached eggs made popular in the Middle East, is one of my absolute favorite breakfasts. This quiche delivers all the same flavors in pie form, making it ideal for sharing and packing up to go.

YIELD
Makes 1 (9-inch [23-cm]) deep-dish quiche

INGREDIENTS
· ½ recipe All-Purpose Dough (page 22), patted into a disc
· 2 tbsp (30 ml) olive oil
· 3 cloves garlic, finely chopped
· 1 small onion, roughly chopped
· 2 tsp (4 g) smoked paprika
· 1 tsp crushed red pepper
· 1 (12-oz [340-g]) jar roasted red peppers, drained and patted dry, roughly chopped
· 1 (14.5-oz [411-g]) can diced tomatoes, drained
· 1 tsp sea salt, plus more for seasoning vegetables
· ½ tsp freshly ground black pepper, plus more for seasoning vegetables
· 6 large eggs, room temperature
· 1¼ cups (300 ml) heavy whipping cream, room temperature
· ½ cup (86 g) crumbled feta cheese
· Roughly chopped fresh tender herbs, such as cilantro, parsley, basil or dill, for serving
· Citrusy Whipped Yogurt (page 176), for serving

DIRECTIONS
Preheat the oven to 375°F (190°C), and line a rimmed baking sheet with parchment paper or foil. On a well-floured surface, roll the dough out to a ¼-inch (6-mm) thick round about 12 inches (30 cm) in diameter. Transfer the dough to a 9-inch (23-cm) deep-dish pie pan and position it so that it's centered with about an inch (2.5 cm) of dough hanging over the sides. Tuck the excess dough underneath itself. Crimp the edges however you'd like using one of the crimping methods (pages 15–16). Prick all over the bottom with a fork, and freeze the crust for 30 minutes.

To blind-bake the crust, cut a piece of parchment paper large enough to fit inside the pie shell and up the sides with a few extra inches of overhang. Crumple up the parchment a few times to soften it. Smooth it out and fit it inside the pie shell. Fill up to the top of the pie with pie weights, dried beans or rice. Bake the shell on the prepared baking sheet for 20 minutes, until the crust is just set, then remove the weights by lifting out the whole piece of parchment. Bake the shell for 15 to 20 minutes, or until the crust is a light brown but the bottom is crisp. Remove the shell from the oven, and reduce the temperature to 325°F (163°C).

Meanwhile, make the filling. In a large skillet heat the olive oil over medium heat, add the garlic and onion and sauté for a few minutes, until the onion is translucent, stirring occasionally. Add the paprika and crushed red pepper, and stir to coat them in the oil. Let the spices bloom for about 30 seconds, then add the roasted red peppers and tomatoes. Season the vegetable mixture generously with salt and pepper and cook, stirring occasionally, until the excess moisture has evaporated, about 5 minutes. Shut off the heat, and set aside the mixture.

In a large bowl, whisk the eggs vigorously to break them up. Whisk in the cream, 1 teaspoon of salt and ½ teaspoon of black pepper. Fold in the feta and cooled tomato and pepper mixture. Pour the filling into the crust. Carefully slide the quiche into the oven, and bake it for 50 to 55 minutes, until the center is set but still wobbles slightly. Cool the quiche completely before slicing it. To serve, sprinkle the quiche with the fresh herbs, and top it with a dollop of the Citrusy Whipped Yogurt.

GREENS, EGGS AND HAM GALETTE WITH CHARRED SCALLIONS AND PANCETTA

This galette is my take on Green Eggs and Ham, *updated with more elevated flavors. The sweetness coaxed out of the charred scallions is the perfect counterpoint to the pleasantly bitter dark greens. The crispy pancetta nuggets add a perfectly salty bite, while the eggs add richness.*

YIELD
Makes 1 (10-inch [25-cm]) galette

INGREDIENTS
· 4 oz (113 g) pancetta, cut into ½-inch (1.3-cm) cubes

· 1 tbsp (15 ml) avocado or other neutral oil

· 1 bunch scallions, ends trimmed

· 1 shallot, peeled and roughly chopped

· 1 bunch Swiss chard, stems cut into ¼-inch (6-mm) pieces and leaves cut into ribbons

· Sea salt

· Freshly ground black pepper

· 1 tbsp (15 ml) apple cider vinegar

· 2 oz (57 g) Parmigiano-Reggiano cheese, grated

· 1 recipe Buttermilk Dough (page 24), patted into 1 large disc

· 1 egg, lightly beaten, plus 3 large whole eggs, divided

· Flaky salt

· Roughly chopped fresh chives, for serving

DIRECTIONS
Line a plate with paper towels. Heat a skillet over medium heat. Add the pancetta and cook, stirring occasionally, until it is crisp and the fat has rendered, 10 to 12 minutes. With a slotted spoon, transfer the pancetta to the prepared plate to drain the fat. Meanwhile, in a cast-iron skillet over medium-high heat, heat the avocado oil until it's smoking. Add the scallions in a single layer, let them get a good char on them, about 2 minutes, then flip them. They'll really sizzle and sputter but that's good! Let the scallions get a char on the other side, about a minute or so. Transfer the scallions to a cutting board to cool slightly.

Turn the heat down to medium; add another drizzle of avocado oil, if necessary. Add the shallot and sauté until it's softened and translucent, 2 minutes or so. Add the Swiss chard stems and cook them for about 2 minutes, just until they're starting to soften. Add the chard leaves, and season the mixture with salt and pepper. Drizzle in the apple cider vinegar and toss to coat. Continue cooking for another minute or so, until the leaves are tender and starting to wilt and the vinegar has reduced. Transfer the Swiss chard mixture to a large bowl. Roughly chop the cooled scallions and add them to the bowl, along with the cheese. Season again with salt and pepper to taste.

Preheat the oven to 400°F (204°C), and line a rimmed baking sheet with parchment paper. On a well-floured work surface, roll the dough out into a ¼- to ⅛-inch (6- to 3-mm) thick round about 12 inches (30 cm) in diameter, then transfer it to the prepared baking sheet. Spread the scallion and chard filling out in the center of the dough in an even layer, leaving about a 2-inch (5-cm) border of dough all around. Sprinkle the pancetta over the filling. Fold up the sides however you'd like using one of the galette fold methods (pages 14–15). Freeze the galette for 30 minutes.

Brush the sides of the dough with the lightly beaten egg, and sprinkle them with the flaky salt. Bake the galette for about 40 minutes, until the crust is golden brown. Take the galette out of the oven. Crack 1 egg into a small bowl, then tip the egg onto the galette. Repeat with the rest of the eggs, spacing them out equidistantly on the galette. Season the eggs with salt and pepper, then bake the galette for 6 to 8 minutes, until the whites of the egg are firm and opaque, but the yolk is still wobbly. Sprinkle the chives over the top of the galette and serve it warm.

FRESH CORN AND HEIRLOOM TOMATO PIE WITH CHEDDAR AND CHIVES

This pie is an unabashed celebration of summer. There's nothing quite like a tomato plucked straight outta the garden, still warm from the summer sun, dressed only with salt. Or biting into a perfect, sweet and crisp ear of corn, butter and juices dripping down your chin. But it's so good you can't be bothered to care. This pie takes that sweet corn and those juicy tomatoes and nestles them into the cheesiest cheddar and chive custard for a truly irresistible combination.

YIELD
Makes 1 (9-inch [23-cm]) pie

INGREDIENTS
· 2 lbs (908 g) heirloom tomatoes, cut into ¼-inch (6-mm) slices

· Sea salt

· Olive oil

· ½ recipe Cheddar Dough (page 25), patted into a disc

· ½ cup (120 ml) crème fraîche, room temperature

· 1 large egg, room temperature

· 2 oz (57 g) extra sharp cheddar cheese, grated

· ½ tsp freshly ground black pepper

· 3 tbsp (9 g) finely chopped fresh chives or chive blossoms, divided

· 2 large ears (200 g) fresh yellow corn, kernels removed, divided

DIRECTIONS
Arrange the tomato slices in a single layer on a rimmed baking sheet. Sprinkle one side of the tomatoes with sea salt, and let them sit for 1 hour.

Preheat the oven to 400°F (204°C). Blot the tomatoes well with a paper towel to soak up the excess moisture that has leached out of them, and transfer them to a dry rimmed baking sheet. Drizzle them with the olive oil, and use your hands to coat both sides of them. Spread them out in an even layer. Roast the tomatoes for 45 to 55 minutes, until they have shrunk, are starting to caramelize and all their juices have reduced. Set aside the tomatoes to cool.

While the tomatoes are roasting, let's roll out and chill the crust and make the filling.

On a well-floured surface, roll the dough out to a ⅛-inch (3-mm) thick round about 12 inches (30 cm) in diameter. Transfer the dough to a 9-inch (23-cm) pie pan, and position it so that it's centered with about an inch (2.5 cm) of dough hanging over the sides. Crimp the edges however you'd like using one of the crimping methods (pages 15–16). Freeze the pie for 30 minutes.

Line a rimmed baking sheet with foil.

Whisk together the crème fraîche, egg, cheddar, pepper and 2 tablespoons (6 g) of the chives. Reserve ¼ cup (50 g) of the corn kernels, then add the rest to the custard and stir to combine. Pour the custard into the pie shell, and layer the roasted tomato slices on top. Sprinkle the reserved corn and remaining 1 tablespoon (3 g) of chives over the tomatoes.

Bake the pie, on the prepared baking sheet, for 40 to 50 minutes, until the crust is deep golden brown. The filling may puff up a little, but that's OK. It'll fall as it cools. Cool the pie for at least 15 minutes before slicing it. This pie may be served warm or at room temperature.

VARIATION: Try this recipe with All-Purpose Dough, herb variation (page 22), using thyme.

ROASTED ZUCCHINI AND SUMMER SQUASH TART

Sometimes simple is best. When you find yourself with an abundance of zucchini or various summer squashes, this is a great way to make use of them. The simple herby ricotta custard is a nice base to hold everything together and lends a mild oniony flavor. Try to find vegetables that are around the same circumference, since they'll be stacked and shingled together in the tart. Feel free to use any tender summer squash.

YIELD
Makes 1 (12-inch [30-cm]) tart

INGREDIENTS
· 1 large or 2 medium zucchini, ends removed and sliced into ¼-inch (6-mm) coins

· 1 large or 2 medium yellow summer squash, ends removed and sliced into ¼-inch (6-mm) coins

· 1 tbsp (15 ml) olive oil, plus more for cooking shallots and garlic

· 2 tsp (2 g) finely chopped fresh thyme

· ¼ tsp sea salt, plus more for seasoning vegetables

· ½ tsp freshly ground black pepper, plus more for seasoning vegetables

· ½ recipe All-Purpose Dough, herb variation (page 22) with thyme, patted into a disc

· 1 large shallot, peeled and thinly sliced

· 2 large cloves garlic, peeled and finely chopped

· ½ cup (113 g) whole milk ricotta cheese, room temperature

· 1 large egg, room temperature

DIRECTIONS

Preheat the oven to 375°F (190°C). Combine the zucchini, summer squash, 1 tablespoon (15 ml) of olive oil and thyme in a large bowl. Season the mixture with salt and pepper, and toss to combine, being sure each piece of vegetable is evenly coated. Lay the vegetables out in a single layer on two rimmed baking sheets. Roast the vegetables for 25 to 30 minutes, rotating the baking sheets halfway through, just until vegetables have shrunk and are just beginning to caramelize around the edges but haven't taken on too much color. Set the vegetables aside to cool.

While the vegetables are roasting, let's prepare the tart shell. On a well-floured surface, roll the dough out into a ⅛-inch (3-mm) thick round, and transfer it to a 12-inch (30 cm) round tart pan with a removable bottom. Drape the dough down the side of the pan so as to not stretch out the dough. Using your thumb, trim away the excess dough by gently pressing the dough against the scalloped edge of the pan. Prick all over the bottom of the dough gently with the tines of a fork. Freeze the tart shell until it's very firm, about 30 minutes.

Line a rimmed baking sheet with parchment paper or foil, and place the tart shell on it. Cut a piece of parchment paper large enough to fit inside the pie shell and up the sides, with a few extra inches (8 cm) of overhang. Crumple up the parchment a few times to soften it. Smooth it out and fit it inside the pie shell. Fill up to the top of the pie with pie weights, dried beans or rice. Bake the shell for 20 to 25 minutes, until the dough is set and starting to get a little color on the edges. Remove the weights and parchment, and bake the shell for 15 to 20 minutes, until it's golden brown and the bottom is crisp.

(continued)

ROASTED ZUCCHINI AND SUMMER SQUASH TART (CONTINUED)

Meanwhile, make the filling while the shell is baking. Heat a small skillet over medium heat. Add a drizzle of the olive oil and the shallot. Season lightly with salt, and sauté for 3 to 5 minutes, or until the shallot has softened, stirring occasionally. Add the garlic, and cook for another minute or so, until fragrant. Remove the pan from the heat and set it aside. In a small bowl, mix together the ricotta, egg, ¼ teaspoon of salt and ½ teaspoon of pepper. Add the garlic and shallot, and stir everything to combine.

Spread the filling in the bottom of the tart shell in an even layer. Now, layer the slices of roasted zucchini and summer squash in a spiral pattern on top of the filling, alternating vegetables.

Reduce the temperature to 350°F (177°C). Bake the tart for 20 to 25 minutes, until the filling is set. Cool the tart for a few minutes before removing it from the tart pan. Serve the tart warm or at room temperature.

VARIATION: Try this recipe with Buttermilk Dough (page 24).

DEEP-DISH BROCCOLI CHEDDAR CHICKEN POT PIE

I wish I could tell you I dreamed up this one, but the genius behind this incredible pie belongs 100 percent to my cousin, Mandy, and she was gracious enough to lend it to me for the book. This has been the chicken pot pie everyone in our family has been making for years, so I had to do a bit of digging to find the origin story. Mandy originally developed it as her entry for the Pillsbury Bake-Off, and they somehow passed it up. All I have to say is, their loss, because it's the chicken pot pie you never knew you needed. Ultravelvety and incredibly cheesy sharp cheddar sauce enrobes all the vegetables and chicken, and crisp-tender broccoli florets, in place of the traditional peas, complement the cheddar so well.

YIELD

Makes 1 (9 x 13 x 2–inch [23 x 33 x 5–cm]) pot pie or 2 (9-inch [23-cm]) deep-dish pies

INGREDIENTS

Filling
· 4 medium boneless, skinless chicken breasts

· Sea salt

· Freshly ground black pepper

· 3 medium Yukon gold potatoes (760 g), cut into ½-inch (1.3-cm) cubes

· 12 large carrots (716 g), cut into ½-inch (1.3-cm) rounds

· 3 cups (175 g) broccoli, cut into ½-inch (1.3-cm) florets

Béchamel
· 6 cups (1.4 L) whole milk

· ¾ cup (168 g) unsalted butter, room temperature

· ¾ cup (94 g) all-purpose flour

· 3½ tsp (18 g) sea salt

· 3 tsp (15 g) freshly ground black pepper

· 1 tbsp (3 g) finely chopped fresh thyme

· 10 oz (283 g) extra sharp cheddar cheese, grated

Crust
· 2 recipes All-Purpose Dough, herb variation (page 22) with thyme, each patted into one large rectangle

· 1 large egg, lightly beaten

· Flaky salt

DIRECTIONS

For the filling, preheat the oven to 375°F (190°C). Season the chicken breasts generously with salt and pepper on both sides. Wrap each tightly in foil in a little parcel, place the parcels on a rimmed baking sheet and bake the breasts for 25 to 30 minutes, or until the internal temperature reaches 165°F (74°C). Leave the oven on to bake the pot pie. Set aside the chicken breasts to cool.

Bring a large pot of water to a boil. Add the potatoes and carrots to the boiling water, and boil them for about 8 minutes, until the carrots and potatoes are both fork-tender but not mushy. Work in batches if necessary, so as not to overcrowd the pot when cooking the vegetables. Remove the vegetables with a slotted spoon, and transfer them to a very large bowl. This will be the bowl all of the filling gets mixed in, so make sure it's nice and big. Now, add the broccoli to the pot and boil it for 1 minute, or until tender, then transfer it to the bowl with the carrots and potatoes, using a slotted spoon. Once the chicken is cool, cut the breasts into ½-inch (1.3-cm) cubes and add them to the vegetables.

(continued)

DEEP-DISH BROCCOLI CHEDDAR CHICKEN POT PIE (CONTINUED)

For the béchamel, heat the milk in a large saucepan over medium heat, until it's warm but not boiling, 3 to 5 minutes. Remove the pan from the heat and set it aside. In a large heavy-bottomed saucepan over medium heat, melt the butter. Add the flour and whisk to combine. Continue to whisk until the mixture has bubbled and the butter smells nutty, about a minute or so. Slowly stream in the warmed milk, whisking constantly. It may initially clump or seize up a bit, but that's OK! Just keep whisking and it will smooth out. Continue to whisk the mixture for 3 to 5 minutes, until it coats the back of a spoon and you can run your finger down the back and have the line stay in place. Add the salt, pepper and thyme, and stir to combine. Remove the pan from the heat and stir in the cheese, whisking until it's melted. Set aside the mixture to cool slightly.

For the crust, line a rimmed baking sheet with foil. On a well-floured surface, roll out the bottom crust into a ⅛-inch (3-mm) thick rectangle large enough to fit into a 9 x 13 x 2–inch (23 x 33 x 5–cm) baking dish with about ½ inch (1.3 cm) of overhang. Roll out the top crust to a ⅛-inch (3-mm) thick rectangle, and set it aside.

To finish the filling, pour the béchamel over the vegetable and chicken mixture, and stir it well to make sure everything is coated evenly. Pour the filling into the baking dish and spread it into an even layer. Choose one of the double-crust topping techniques, such as the classic lattice (page 18), and top the filling with the top crust, rerolling any scraps leftover once, if necessary. Brush the top crust with the beaten egg and sprinkle it with the flaky salt.

Place the baking dish on the prepared baking sheet, and bake the pot pie for 65 to 75 minutes, until the crust is deep golden brown and the filling is bubbling. Cool the pot pie for about 15 minutes before slicing and serving it.

VARIATION: Try this recipe with Cheddar Dough (page 25).

HOT TIP: This recipe also fits perfectly into two 9-inch (23-cm) deep-dish pie pans if you'd rather make a smaller portion. It's perfect for making one to serve now and stashing the other, fully assembled and unbaked, in the freezer for a rainy day or giving to a friend or neighbor. Pop the pie in the oven, adding 15 minutes of baking time for a frozen pie. The only adjustment you'll need to make to the recipe, other than splitting the filling evenly between the two pies, is to pat each recipe of dough into two discs (one each for top and bottom of each pie) rather than a large, single rectangle.

ROASTED CHERRY TOMATO BLOODY MARY GALETTE

If you love the spicy zip of a Bloody Mary, this is the pie for you. It's got all the flavors of the cocktail, conveniently wrapped up in a pie parcel. While this pie is a wonderful opportunity to take advantage of summer's best tomatoes, roasting the tomatoes coaxes out sweetness and umami from even the most subpar tomatoes.

YIELD
Makes 1 (10-inch [25-cm]) galette

INGREDIENTS
· 2 lbs (908 g) cherry tomatoes, any color, halved

· 1 tbsp (15 ml) olive oil

· Sea salt

· 1 cup (226 g) whole milk ricotta cheese

· Zest of 1 lemon, finely grated

· 1 tbsp (15 ml) freshly squeezed lemon juice

· 1½ tsp (8 ml) Worcestershire sauce

· 1 tsp Tabasco® or other vinegary hot sauce

· 1 tsp prepared horseradish

· ½ tsp celery salt

· ½ tsp freshly ground black pepper

· 1 recipe Buttermilk Dough (page 24), patted into 1 large disc

· 1 egg, lightly beaten

· ½ tsp celery seeds

· Roughly chopped fresh tender herbs, such as basil, chives or parsley, for serving

DIRECTIONS
Preheat the oven to 400°F (204°C).

Arrange the tomatoes in a single layer on a rimmed baking sheet, drizzle them with the olive oil and season them lightly with salt. Roast the tomatoes for about 30 minutes, until they are shriveled and starting to brown in a few places and all their juices have reduced. Set the tomatoes aside to cool while you assemble the filling.

In a large bowl, combine the ricotta, lemon zest, lemon juice, Worcestershire sauce, Tabasco, horseradish, celery salt and pepper, and stir to combine.

Line a rimmed baking sheet with parchment paper. On a well-floured work surface, roll the dough out into a ¼-inch (6-mm) thick round about 12 inches (30 cm) in diameter, and place it on the baking sheet. Spread the ricotta mixture out in the center of the dough in an even layer, leaving about a 2-inch (5-cm) border of dough all around. Layer the tomatoes on top, and fold up the sides of the dough around the filling however you'd like using one of the galette fold methods (pages 14–15). Freeze the galette for 30 minutes.

Brush the crust with the beaten egg and sprinkle it with the celery seeds. Bake the galette for 45 to 50 minutes, until the crust is a deep golden brown. Sprinkle the galette with the fresh herbs, and serve it warm or at room temperature.

VARIATION: Try this recipe with the All-Purpose Dough (page 22), black pepper variation.

BACON, DATE AND GOAT CHEESE TART

On Christmas Eve, our family usually opts for a spread of fun appetizers and hors d'oeuvres rather than a formal dinner. By far the most popular dish every year are my mom's bacon-wrapped dates stuffed with goat cheese. From the time they come out of the oven, they seem to disappear in a matter of minutes: no wonder, with the irresistible sweet, salty and creamy combination. This tart is a perfect expression of the very best appetizer in pie form.

YIELD
Makes 1 (14 x 4–inch [36 x 10–cm]) tart

INGREDIENTS
· ½ recipe All-Purpose Dough (page 22), patted into a rectangle
· 6 large, soft Medjool dates (130 g), pitted and halved
· Boiling water
· 6 oz (170 g) chèvre goat cheese, room temperature
· ½ cup (120 ml) heavy whipping cream, room temperature
· 1 large egg, room temperature
· ½ tsp sea salt
· ¼ tsp freshly ground black pepper
· 3 slices cooked crispy bacon (45 g), crumbled

HOT TIP: For a vegetarian and equally delicious tart, swap the bacon out for ½ cup (80 g) of roughly chopped salted smoked almonds.

VARIATION: Try this recipe with Any-Nut Dough (page 27), using almonds.

DIRECTIONS
Preheat the oven to 375°F (190°C), and line a rimmed baking sheet with parchment paper or foil.

On a well-floured surface, roll the dough out into a ¼- to ⅛-inch (6- to 3-mm) thick rectangle and transfer it to a 14 x 4–inch (36 x 10–cm) tart pan with a removable bottom. Drape the dough down the side of the pan so as to not stretch out the dough. Using your thumb, trim away the excess dough by gently pressing the dough against the scalloped edge of the pan. Prick all over the bottom and sides of the dough gently with the tines of a fork. Freeze the tart shell for about 30 minutes, or until very firm.

Place the tart shell on the prepared baking sheet. Cut a piece of parchment paper large enough to fit inside the pie shell and up the sides, with a few extra inches of overhang. Crumple up the parchment a few times to soften it. Smooth it out and fit it inside the pie shell. Fill up to the top of the pie with pie weights, dried beans or rice. Bake the shell for 15 to 20 minutes, until the dough is set. Remove the weights and parchment, and bake the shell for 10 to 15 minutes, until it's golden brown and the bottom is crisp. Set the shell aside to cool on the baking sheet. Reduce the oven temperature to 350°F (177°C).

Pulse the dates and 2 tablespoons (30 ml) of boiling water in a food processor until a thick but spreadable paste forms, 2 to 3 minutes. If your dates are a bit firmer or on the drier side, you may need to add a bit more water to get the desired consistency. Keeping the tart pan on the rimmed baking sheet, use an offset spatula to spread the date mixture evenly on the bottom of the cooled shell. Wipe out the food processor, and add the goat cheese, cream, egg, salt and pepper; process until the mixture is smooth, about 30 seconds. Pour the filling over the date mixture. Sprinkle the bacon all over the filling. Bake the tart for 25 to 30 minutes, until the filling is firm and set and just starting to turn a bit golden in spots. This tart may be served warm or at room temperature.

KALE AND ARTICHOKE GALETTE

OK, to be clear: this is essentially an artichoke dip in pie form, and I don't think there's anything wrong with that. On the contrary, there's a lot of things right with it. When I moved into my first apartment, I threw a housewarming party and went a little overboard with the snacks; I made a feast for about 20 instead of the small group of friends I'd invited—no regrets. By far, the favorite of the evening was the giant skillet of bubbling, cheesy spinach and artichoke dip. If you've had it, it's pretty irresistible, so no surprise there. Here, I've elevated the classic dip just a bit and swapped kale in place of spinach for a heartier, earthier flavor that holds its own against the creamy, tangy filling, which has plenty of salty Parmigiano and tender artichoke hearts.

YIELD
Makes about an 8-inch (20-cm) galette

INGREDIENTS
Filling
- 4 oz (113 g) full-fat cream cheese, room temperature
- ½ cup (120 ml) full-fat sour cream, room temperature
- 1 large egg, room temperature
- 5 oz (140 g) Parmigiano-Reggiano cheese, finely grated, divided
- 3 tbsp (45 ml) white wine vinegar, divided
- 1 tbsp (15 ml) olive oil , plus more if needed
- 1 small onion, roughly chopped
- 2 cloves garlic, finely chopped
- Sea salt
- 2 (14-oz [396-g]) cans canned artichoke hearts, drained and quartered
- Freshly ground black pepper
- 1 small bunch lacinato kale, stemmed and roughly chopped

Crust
- ½ recipe Any-Nut Dough (page 27), using almonds, patted into a disc
- 1 large egg, lightly beaten
- Flaky salt

DIRECTIONS
For the filling, in a large bowl, whisk together the cream cheese, sour cream, egg, 4 ounces (113 g) of the Parmigiano-Reggiano and 2 tablespoons (30 ml) of the vinegar; set aside the mixture.

Heat the olive oil in a large skillet over medium heat. Add the onion and garlic, season lightly with salt, and cook until the garlic is fragrant and the onion is translucent and starting to brown in a few places, 5 to 7 minutes, stirring occasionally. Add the artichoke hearts, and season the mixture well with salt and pepper. Cook until the water from the artichoke hearts has evaporated and they're starting to take on a bit of color, 5 minutes or so. Add the artichokes to the cheese mixture.

Add another drizzle of oil to the skillet and add the kale. Toss, allowing the kale to wilt a minute or two. Drizzle in the remaining tablespoon (15 ml) of the vinegar; toss to combine. Cook for another minute or so, then add the kale to the artichoke and cheese mixture. Stir everything to combine the ingredients. Allow the filling to cool to room temperature.

(continued)

KALE AND ARTICHOKE GALETTE (CONTINUED)

For the crust, preheat the oven to 400°F (204°C), and line a rimmed baking sheet with parchment paper. On a well-floured surface, roll the dough out into a large round ¼ to ⅛ inch (6 to 3 mm) thick and 10 to 12 inches (25 to 30 cm) in diameter. Transfer the dough to the prepared baking sheet. Place the filling in the middle in an even layer, leaving about a 2-inch (5-cm) border around the whole galette. Fold up the sides around the filling, and sprinkle the remaining 1 ounce (27 g) of Parmigiano on the filling. Freeze the galette for 30 minutes.

Brush the dough with the beaten egg and sprinkle it with the flaky salt. Bake the galette for 40 to 45 minutes, until the filling is firm and bubbly, the cheese is golden and the crust is a deep golden brown. Cool the galette slightly before slicing it.

VARIATION: Try this recipe with Buckwheat Dough (page 29).

BEEF BOURGUIGNON SKILLET PIE

I adore the rich and comforting flavors of beef bourguignon, so I set out to create a pie version that delivered that same coziness. I found this skillet version with only a top crust was just the ticket. The deep umami of beef and red wine flavors, combined with the aromatic herbes de Provence and sweet, tender vegetables, balance nicely with a buttery, flaky lid. Serve warm with a lovely glass of wine on a chilly winter evening.

YIELD
Makes 1 (10-inch [25-cm]) skillet pie

INGREDIENTS
- 4 slices bacon, cut into ½-inch (1.3-cm) pieces
- Sea salt
- Freshly ground black pepper
- 1 lb (454 g) chuck roast, cut into 1-inch (2.5-cm) cubes
- 2 tbsp (28 g) unsalted butter, room temperature
- 1 (14-oz [396-g]) bag frozen pearl onions, thawed and drained, or 1 large white onion, roughly chopped
- 6 medium carrots, cut on the bias into 1-inch (2.5-cm) slices
- 1 tbsp (3 g) dried herbes de Provence
- 3 cloves garlic, finely chopped
- 1 tbsp (20 g) tomato paste
- 1 tbsp (15 ml) Worcestershire sauce
- 3 tbsp (24 g) all-purpose flour
- 2 cups (480 ml) dry red wine, such as Pinot Noir
- 1 cup (240 ml) beef stock
- ½ recipe All-Purpose Dough, herb variation (page 22) with thyme, patted into a disc
- 1 egg, lightly beaten
- Flaky salt
- Roughly chopped fresh tender herbs, such as parsley, tarragon or chives, for serving

DIRECTIONS
In a large, cast-iron Dutch oven or heavy-bottomed pot with a lid, sauté the bacon over medium heat, until the fat has rendered and the bacon is crispy, 5 to 7 minutes. Use a slotted spoon to transfer the bacon to a plate. Salt and pepper the beef generously on both sides, then add half to the pot in a single layer, with a bit of room in between the pieces to allow them to brown rather than steam. Cook, letting the beef brown on one side, 3 to 4 minutes. Flip and brown on the second side, 3 minutes or so. Remove the beef using the slotted spoon, and add it to the plate with the bacon. Repeat with the rest of the beef, and transfer the second batch to the plate.

Melt the butter, and add the onions, carrots and herbes de Provence and cook for 7 to 9 minutes, stirring occasionally, until the vegetables start to brown. Add the garlic and stir to combine, letting it cook for about a minute. Add the tomato paste and Worcestershire sauce, and cook for about a minute, letting the tomato paste coat all the vegetables and turn a dark brick red, stirring constantly. Add the beef and bacon, along with any juices left on the plate. Sprinkle in the flour, and stir to coat the vegetables and beef with it. Pour in the wine and beef stock, and use a wooden spoon to scrape up all the bits at the bottom of the pot. Turn the heat down to medium-low, cover the pan and cook the stew for 2 hours, until the liquid has thickened and reduced, stirring occasionally.

Transfer the stew to a 10-inch (25-cm) ovenproof skillet, such as cast-iron or stainless steel, and set it aside to cool while you prepare the crust.

(continued)

BEEF BOURGUIGNON SKILLET PIE (CONTINUED)

Line a rimmed baking sheet with parchment paper or foil. Roll the dough out onto a well-floured work surface into a ¼-inch (6-mm) thick round, about 10 to 12 inches (25 to 30 cm) in diameter. The round should just fit over the filling on the skillet and go to the edge of the pan. The size will differ slightly depending on the pan you're using and its slope. Transfer the round to the prepared baking sheet.

To make the laurel leaf and branch design, roll out two long ropes of dough, using the scraps of dough. Curve the ropes along each side of the round to make the branches, placing them about an inch (2.5 cm) from the edges with a bit of space at both the top and bottom. Reroll any remaining scraps to a ¼-inch (6-mm) thickness. Use a small leaf cookie cutter or a paring knife to cut out leaves. Use a paring knife to cut a shallow slit along the middle of the leaf, being careful not to cut all the way through it. Arrange the leaves on the branches however you'd like, gently patting them into the dough to adhere. Alternatively, for a simpler design, skip the laurel leaf and branch decoration and simply cut a few vent holes in the crust when you are ready to bake the pie.

Place the baking sheet with the dough in the freezer for 30 minutes. Preheat the oven to 400°F (204°C).

Place the frozen crust on top of the filling in the skillet, pressing it in gently, if necessary, so it fits snugly against the filling. Brush the top of the crust with the beaten egg, cut a few vent holes along the side of a few of the leaves with a sharp paring knife so they're inconspicuous and sprinkle on the flaky salt. Place the skillet on the prepared baking sheet the dough was freezing on.

Bake the pie for 35 to 40 minutes, until the crust is deep golden brown. Allow the pie to cool for a few minutes, sprinkle it with the herbs and serve it.

ROASTED APPLE, ONION AND CABBAGE GALETTE WITH CARAWAY

This Nordic-inspired galette is a simple and soul-satisfying combination. Roasting the apples and vegetables brings out their sweetness and brings a caramelized quality to them, adding depth to the apples and onions, and mellowing the bitter bite of cabbage. The addition of caraway adds that distinct, mild, earthy anise flavor that pairs so well with these lovely winter vegetables.

YIELD
Makes 1 (10-inch [25-cm]) galette

INGREDIENTS
· 1 small head green cabbage, cored and cut into 8 wedges

· 2 firm, tart apples, such as Granny Smith, peeled, cored and cut into 1-inch (2.5-cm) wedges

· 1 large white or yellow onion, halved from root to stem end, then cut into 1-inch (2.5-cm) wedges

· ¼ cup (60 ml) olive oil

· Sea salt

· Freshly ground black pepper

· 2 tsp (5 g) caraway seeds

· 1 recipe Brown Butter Dough (page 23), patted into one large disc

· 1 egg, lightly beaten

· Flaky salt

DIRECTIONS
Preheat the oven to 400°F (204°C). In a large bowl, toss the cabbage, apples and onion to combine. Drizzle them with the olive oil, season them with salt and pepper and sprinkle in the caraway seeds. Toss everything to combine the ingredients. Transfer the mixture to a rimmed sheet pan, and spread it in a single layer. Roast the mixture for 35 to 40 minutes, until everything is tender and caramelized, flipping everything halfway through the roasting time. Cool the mixture to room temperature.

Line a rimmed baking sheet with parchment paper. On a well-floured work surface, roll the dough out into a ¼-inch (6-mm) thick round about 12 inches (30 cm) in diameter. Transfer the dough to the prepared baking sheet. Arrange the vegetables in the center of the dough, layering them if necessary and leaving about a 2-inch (5-cm) border on all sides. Fold up the edges around the filling, brush the crust with the beaten egg and sprinkle it with flaky salt. Bake for 45 to 50 minutes, until the crust is deep golden brown. Serve warm.

VARIATION: Try this recipe with Rye Dough (page 26).

BUTTERNUT SQUASH, SAGE AND BROWN BUTTER GALETTE

If you were to capture the flavor of fall and put it in a pie, this would be it. I can't think of anything quite as autumnal as the sweet flavor of a perfect butternut squash. The earthy sage and nutty brown butter crust round out the sweet squash and make for a truly scrumptious little pie. A slice of this is perfect on its own or paired with a roast chicken for a cozy fall gathering.

YIELD
Makes 1 (10-inch [25-cm]) galette

INGREDIENTS
· 2 lbs (908 g) butternut squash, peeled and cut into ⅛-inch (3-mm) slices, stem end in rounds and bulb end in half-moons; I use a mandolin for this

· 2 tbsp (6 g) finely chopped fresh sage

· 4 cloves garlic, finely chopped

· 1 large shallot, thinly sliced

· ¼ cup (60 ml) olive oil

· Sea salt

· Freshly ground black pepper

· 1 recipe Brown Butter Dough (page 23), patted into 1 large disc

· 1 egg, lightly beaten

· Flaky salt

DIRECTIONS
Preheat the oven to 400°F (204°C), and arrange racks in the middle and bottom of the oven. In a large bowl, combine the squash, sage, garlic, shallot and olive oil. Season the mixture generously with salt and pepper, and toss well to combine the ingredients. Divide the squash mixture evenly between two rimmed baking sheets, and spread it in a single layer. Place one baking sheet on the middle rack and the other on the lower rack. Roast the squash for 20 to 25 minutes, until it's tender and some of the slices are starting to brown and curl around the edges; rotate the sheets halfway through the cooking time. Allow the squash to get cool to the touch before adding it to the crust.

Line a rimmed baking sheet with parchment paper. Roll the dough out into a ¼- to ⅛-inch (6- to 3-mm) thick round and transfer it to the prepared baking sheet. Arrange the slices of squash in a circular pattern in the center of the dough, leaving about a 2-inch (5-cm) border of dough all around. I like to layer the half-moons underneath and place the full rounds on top. Fold up the sides however you'd like using one of the galette fold methods (pages 14–15). Freeze the galette for 30 minutes.

Brush the sides of the dough with the beaten egg and sprinkle them with the flaky salt. Bake the galette for 40 to 45 minutes, until the crust is deep golden brown. Allow the galette to cool for a few minutes before serving it.

CRANBERRY, BRIE AND WALNUT TART WITH ROSEMARY

Inspired by brie en croute, this delicious little tart is wonderful served alongside a bubbly cocktail and other appetizers for a festive holiday fete. Gooey, melted brie is topped with tart cranberries, crisp walnuts, sticky honey and a shower of fresh rosemary all encased in a crisp rosemary crust. What's not to like?

YIELD
Makes 1 (14 x 4–inch [36 x 10–cm]) tart

INGREDIENTS
· ½ recipe All-Purpose Dough, herb variation (page 22) with rosemary, patted into a rectangle
· 1 cup (110 g) fresh or thawed frozen whole cranberries
· ⅓ cup (36 g) walnuts, toasted and roughly chopped
· 3 tbsp (45 ml) honey
· 1 tsp finely chopped fresh rosemary
· ½ tsp sea salt
· ½ tsp freshly ground black pepper
· 4 oz (113 g) brie cheese, cut into ¼-inch (6-mm) thick slices

DIRECTIONS
Preheat the oven to 375°F (190°C), and line a rimmed baking sheet with parchment paper or foil. On a well-floured surface, roll the dough out into a ⅛-inch (3-mm) thick rectangle. Transfer it to a 14 x 4–inch (36 x 10–cm) tart pan with a removable bottom. Drape the dough down the side of the pan so as to not stretch out the dough. Using your thumb, trim away the excess dough by gently pressing the dough against the scalloped edge of the pan. Prick all over the bottom and sides of the dough gently with the tines of a fork. Freeze the tart shell for about 30 minutes, until it's very firm.

Place the tart shell on the prepared baking sheet. Cut a piece of parchment paper large enough to fit inside the pie shell and up the sides, with a few extra inches of overhang. Crumple up the parchment a few times to soften it. Smooth it out and fit it inside the pie shell. Fill up to the top of the pie with pie weights, dried beans or rice. Bake the shell for 15 to 20 minutes, until the dough is set. Remove the weights and parchment, and bake the shell for 10 to 15 minutes, until it's just starting to turn a light golden.

While the shell is baking, make the filling. Combine the cranberries, walnuts, honey, rosemary, salt and pepper in a bowl, and toss to coat the ingredients. Lay the brie slices side by side in the bottom of the par-baked tart shell, so the whole bottom is covered. Pour the cranberry mixture on top. Bake the tart for 20 to 25 minutes, until the cheese is melted and bubbly and the cranberries are thick and jammy. Cool the tart for a few minutes, then slice it and serve it warm.

VARIATION: Try this recipe with Buckwheat Dough (page 29).

THINK SCRAPPY! Have some leftover dough scraps? Put them to good use with a recipe from the Waste Not, Want Not chapter (page 181).

CARAMELIZED ONION AND GRUYÈRE GALETTE

If you love French onion soup, with its rich, beefy broth, sweet, deeply caramelized onions, and that luscious, nutty and gooey layer of cheese-laden toast, you'll love this galette. All the flavors of the classic soup have been distilled into a galette for ease, but also for fun! I love to serve this as a hearty fall or winter dinner alongside a fresh, green salad simply dressed with some red wine vinegar and good olive oil. Bon appétit.

YIELD
Makes about an 8-inch (20-cm) galette

INGREDIENTS
· 1 tbsp (15 ml) olive oil
· 1 tbsp (14 g) unsalted butter, room temperature
· 1 large white or yellow onion, cut into ¼-inch (6-mm) thick rounds with layers intact
· 3 whole sprigs fresh thyme plus 5 sprigs with leaves removed from stems and finely chopped, divided
· 3 whole sprigs fresh rosemary plus 2 sprigs with leaves removed from stems and finely chopped, divided
· Sea salt
· Freshly ground black pepper
· ½ cup (120 ml) red wine, whatever you enjoy drinking
· ¼ cup (60 ml) beef broth
· 4 oz (113 g) Gruyère cheese, grated
· 1 oz (28 g) Parmigiano-Reggiano cheese, grated
· ½ recipe Rye Dough (page 26), patted into a disc
· 1 egg, lightly beaten
· Flaky salt

DIRECTIONS

Heat a large cast-iron skillet over medium-low heat. Add the olive oil and butter to the skillet. Once the butter has melted, add the onion rounds in a single layer and tuck the whole sprigs of rosemary and thyme around the skillet. Season the onion with salt and pepper and let it cook, undisturbed, for about 10 minutes, until the onion is caramelized and golden brown on the bottom. Carefully flip, being careful to keep the onions in one piece, season with salt and pepper again, and cook for 10 minutes or so, until there's a caramelized layer on the other side. Should you have a few layers of onion slip around a bit, no matter. Just tuck them in their round as best you can. Add the wine and beef broth, and cook until the liquid has reduced and is thick, 5 to 8 minutes. Remove the pan from the heat, and set it aside to cool the onions completely.

In a small bowl, toss the Gruyère and Parmigiano cheeses together with the chopped thyme and rosemary; set aside the bowl.

Line a rimmed baking sheet with parchment paper. On a well-floured surface, roll the dough out into a large circle ¼ to ⅛ inch (6 to 3 mm) thick and 10 to 12 inches (25 to 30 cm) in diameter. Transfer the dough to the prepared baking sheet. Sprinkle the cheese mixture on the dough, leaving about a 2-inch (5-cm) border around the whole thing. Gently arrange the onion rounds over the cheese mixture in a single layer. Spoon the syrupy pan juices over the onions. Fold up the sides of the dough however you'd like using one of the galette fold methods (pages 14–15). Freeze the galette on the baking sheet for 30 minutes.

Meanwhile, preheat the oven to 400°F (204°C). Brush the sides of the dough with the beaten egg, and sprinkle it with the flaky salt. Bake for 30 to 35 minutes, or until the crust is golden brown and the filling is bubbling. Cool the galette for a few minutes before serving it.

VARIATION: Try this recipe with Buckwheat Dough (page 29).

SMALL BUT MIGHTY

While presenting a life-sized pie at any number of gatherings is impressive in its own right and has its place and time, there's just something kinda magical about everyone getting their own little personal parcel. A mini pot pie makes guests feel special. I have always had a fascination with all things miniature and thus irresistible—RIP, all the Polly Pockets of my youth sucked up in the vacuum—so, naturally, this would be my favorite chapter. Just have a look at the petite Rhubarb, Ginger and Goat Cheese Pop-Tarts (page 139) with their soft blush glaze and you'll understand.

And sure, mini galettes and hand pies rank high on the scale of cuteness, but the perfect, single-serve portion is also practical and utilitarian in their portability. Pizza-Vibe Hand Pies with Salami, Fennel and Fontina (page 147) are perfect for toting to friends with new babies. Blackberry Thyme Turnovers (page 152) are ideal for birthdays and picnics. Taking the time to fry up a batch of Strawberry Angostura Hand Pies (page 145) for someone surely says, "I love you, like a lot."

In this chapter, you'll find full meals, snacks, sweet treats and everything in between. Spring Pea Pesto Ricotta Tartlets with Lemon and Crispy Shallots (page 141) make an elegant lunch, while Lil' Smoky Sausage Rolls with Hot and Sweet Mustard (page 168) are a childhood throwback everyone will adore on game night. For an idyllic wintery morning treat to enjoy with your coffee, make a batch of Swedish Cardamom Roll Hand Pies (page 163), and enjoy the warm, cozy scents filling up your home.

The following recipes are an exercise in just how much flavor can be stuffed into a small package. Spoiler: a whole heck of a lot.

RHUBARB, GINGER AND GOAT CHEESE POP-TARTS

This recipe, inspired by a now sadly closed little bakery I once came across in Portland, is one of the most popular I've ever shared on my blog. These little gems are so good, I decided they had to be included in the book. There's just something irresistible about the mouth-puckering, tart rhubarb filling with a hint of spicy ginger that's a wonderful counterpoint to the creamy, tangy goat cheese. Tuck that scrumptious filling into a buttery little parcel, drizzle it with a bit of rhubarb-dyed pink glaze for a perfect balance of sweet and tangy, and you've got yourself the best homemade pop-tart. And, to think, if my sister and I hadn't stumbled into that bakery on our way to see Bon Iver in Portland, these little delights might have never made it into the world.

YIELD
Makes 9 (3 x 4–inch [7 x 10–cm]) pop-tarts

INGREDIENTS
Filling
- 2 cups (300 g) roughly chopped fresh rhubarb, about 4–6 stalks
- 1 tbsp (15 g) finely grated fresh ginger
- ¾ cup (150 g) granulated sugar
- Zest of 1 lemon, finely grated
- Juice of 1 lemon
- Pinch of sea salt
- 2 tbsp (18 g) cornstarch
- 2 tbsp (30 ml) cold water
- 1 tsp vanilla bean paste
- 9 tbsp (90 g) chèvre goat cheese, room temperature

Crust
- 1 recipe All-Purpose Dough (page 22), patted into two rectangles
- 1 egg, lightly beaten

Glaze
- 1 cup (125 g) powdered sugar
- Sprinkles of choice

DIRECTIONS

For the filling, in a medium saucepan over medium heat, stir to combine the rhubarb, ginger, granulated sugar, lemon zest, lemon juice and salt. Continue to stir the mixture occasionally, until it comes to a boil. At this point, the cooking juices should be a deep magenta, but the rhubarb hasn't yet broken down. Spoon out 1 tablespoon (15 ml) of the rhubarb juices, and reserve it for the glaze. Turn the heat down to medium-low, and cook the mixture for 10 to 15 minutes, until the rhubarb has broken down and is soft and the juices have thickened. In a small bowl, stir together the cornstarch and water to make a slurry. Slowly drizzle the slurry mixture into the rhubarb mixture while stirring constantly. Let the mixture bubble for 1 minute, stirring constantly, until it thickens. Remove it from the heat, stir in the vanilla bean paste and allow the mixture to cool completely.

For the crust, preheat the oven to 350°F (177°C), and line a rimmed baking sheet with parchment paper.

(continued)

RHUBARB, GINGER AND GOAT CHEESE POP-TARTS (CONTINUED)

Working with only one rectangle of dough at a time, roll it out onto a lightly floured work surface into a large rectangle about ⅛ inch (3 mm) thick. We want to end up with a 12 x 9–inch (30 by 23–cm) rectangle with straight edges, so roll it just large enough to trim it down to this size. Trim the edges, using a ruler or something with a straight edge and a pizza cutter or sharp knife. Use the ruler and a knife to score the shorter sides at the 3- and 6-inch (8- and 15-cm) marks and the longer sides at the 4- and 8-inch (10- and 20-cm) marks. Use the marks to line up your ruler or straight edge, and cut the dough into nine 3 x 4–inch (8 x 10–cm) rectangles. Transfer the rectangles to the prepared baking sheet, spacing them about an inch (2.5 cm) apart. Freeze the rectangles while you make nine more rectangles with the second rectangle of dough.

Pull out the baking sheet from the freezer, and spread 1 tablespoon (10 g) of goat cheese in the center of each rectangle, leaving about ½ inch (1.3 cm) around all sides. Top the cheese with 1 tablespoon (17 g) of the rhubarb filling, then spread it out slightly to cover the goat cheese. Brush the edges of the rectangle with some of the beaten egg, reserving some for the tops of the tarts, and top it with another rectangle. Press the edges down firmly with your fingers to seal. Crimp the sides with a fork to enclose the tarts. Freeze the tarts for 30 minutes.

Brush the tops of the tarts with the beaten egg. Using a toothpick or paring knife, poke a few holes on the top to allow steam to escape while they bake. Bake the tarts for 30 to 35 minutes, until the crust is golden brown. Cool the tarts completely before glazing them.

To make the glaze, whisk together the powdered sugar and reserved rhubarb juice, adding a few drops of water, a little at a time, if necessary, to reach the desired consistency. It should be thin enough to drizzle but still fairly thick, like honey. Drizzle the glaze over the pop-tarts and top them with the sprinkles.

HOT TIP: Any extra rhubarb filling is delicious on oatmeal or pancakes.

SPRING PEA PESTO RICOTTA TARTLETS WITH LEMON AND CRISPY SHALLOTS

Here is some proof that pie does not always mean heavy and butter-laden. Creamy, verdant and bright pea pesto swirled into ricotta and topped with a bracing and crunchy fresh salad make these a true celebration of spring and all its offerings. These would make a beautiful, light spring lunch. Use the leftover pesto to toss with warm pasta, spread on toast or dip fresh vegetables in.

YIELD
Makes 6 (4-inch [10-cm]) tarts

INGREDIENTS
Crust
· 1 recipe All-Purpose Dough (page 22), patted into one large rectangle

Pea Pesto
· 1 cup (163 g) shelled fresh English peas
· 1 cup (28 g) packed fresh basil
· ¼ cup (15 g) packed fresh mint
· ½ cup (78 g) pine nuts, toasted
· 1 oz (28 g) Parmigiano-Reggiano, grated
· Juice of 1 lemon
· ⅓ cup (80 ml) extra-virgin olive oil
· Sea salt

Filling
· ½ cup (120 g) pea pesto
· ½ cup (120 g) whole milk ricotta cheese
· Zest of 1 lemon, finely grated

Salad
· ¼ cup (60 ml) olive oil
· 2 shallots, thinly sliced into rings
· 4 oz (113 g) fresh snap peas, cut on the bias into ¼-inch (6-mm) slices
· 4 small radishes, very thinly sliced
· 2 tbsp (10 g) pine nuts, toasted
· Handful fresh mint, torn
· Handful fresh basil, torn
· 1 tbsp (15 ml) freshly squeezed lemon juice
· Sea salt
· Freshly ground black pepper

DIRECTIONS
Preheat the oven to 375°F (190°C), and line a rimmed baking sheet with parchment paper.

On a well-floured surface, roll the dough out into a ⅛-inch (3-mm) thick rectangle. Use a 4-inch (10-cm) round tart pan with a removable bottom to trace six circles with a paring knife, cutting each about an inch (2.5 cm) larger than the circumference of the tart pan. Drape the dough down the side of each pan so as to not stretch out the dough. Using your thumb, trim away the excess dough by gently pressing the dough against the scalloped edge of the pan. Prick all over the bottom and sides of each tart gently with the tines of a fork. Arrange the tarts on the prepared baking sheet; freeze the tarts for about 30 minutes, until the crust is very firm.

Cut pieces of parchment paper large enough to fit inside the tart shells and up the sides, with some overhang. Crumple up the parchment a few times to soften it. Smooth it out and fit it inside the tart shells. Fill up to the top of the shells with pie weights, dried beans or rice. Bake the tarts for 15 to 20 minutes, until the dough is set. Remove the weights and parchment, and bake them for 10 to 15 minutes, until the crust is golden brown and the bottoms are crisp. Set aside the shells to cool completely.

(continued)

SPRING PEA PESTO RICOTTA TARTLETS WITH LEMON AND CRISPY SHALLOTS (CONTINUED)

Meanwhile, make the pesto. In a food processor or high-powered blender, process the peas, basil, mint, pine nuts, Parmigiano and lemon juice until a paste forms, 30 seconds to 1 minute. Scrape down the sides of the bowl. With the food processor running, stream the olive oil through the feed tube until the mixture emulsifies, another minute or so. Taste the pesto and season with salt if necessary, depending on the saltiness of the Parmigiano.

For the filling, place ½ cup (120 g) of the pesto in a medium bowl. Add the ricotta cheese and lemon zest; mix well and set aside the bowl. The remaining pesto can be refrigerated in an airtight container for up to 1 week.

For the salad, cook the olive oil and shallots in a small skillet over medium heat, stirring occasionally, until the shallots are crisp and golden brown, 12 to 15 minutes. Watch them carefully; once they start to turn color, they can burn quickly. Remove the shallots with a slotted spoon, and set them aside to cool. They'll continue to get a bit more golden and crisper as they sit. Reserve the oil in another bowl.

In a small bowl, combine the snap peas, radishes, pine nuts, mint, basil, lemon juice and 1 tablespoon (15 ml) of the reserved shallot oil. Season with salt and pepper; toss to combine.

To assemble, divide the pesto and ricotta mixture evenly among the tart shells, and spread it in an even layer. Top each with a generous handful of the salad, then the crispy shallots; serve immediately.

VARIATION: Try this recipe with Buttermilk Dough (page 24).

THINK SCRAPPY! Have some leftover dough scraps? Put them to good use with a recipe from the Waste Not, Want Not chapter (page 181).

STRAWBERRY ANGOSTURA HAND PIES

When you can get your hands on a good pint or two of spring's best strawberries, give these little hand pies a go. The crispy, fried shells lacquered in glaze are reminiscent of a treat you'd get at the county fair. The sweet, strawberry jam filling is really special, thanks to a bit of angostura bitters borrowed from the bar cart to add depth and dimension. Any leftover filling makes a wonderful jam on toast, pancakes or French toast. Or, you can eat it by the spoonful.

YIELD
Makes 10 (5-inch [13-cm]) hand pies

INGREDIENTS
Filling
· 1 lb (454 g) fresh strawberries, roughly chopped
· 1 cup (200 g) granulated sugar
· Zest of 1 lemon, finely grated
· Juice of 1 lemon
· Pinch of sea salt
· 2 tbsp (18 g) cornstarch
· 2 tbsp (30 ml) cold water
· 1 tbsp (15 ml) angostura bitters

Crust
· 1 recipe All-Purpose Dough (page 22), patted into two discs
· Neutral oil for frying, such as vegetable or peanut

Glaze
· 1 cup (130 g) powdered sugar
· 2 tbsp (30 ml) whole milk or half-and-half
· Pinch of sea salt

DIRECTIONS
For the filling, in a large, heavy-bottomed saucepan over medium heat, combine the strawberries, sugar, lemon zest, lemon juice and salt. Cook the mixture, stirring occasionally to combine ingredients and allow the sugar to dissolve. Once the sugar has dissolved, 5 minutes or so, turn the heat up to medium-high, and let the mixture simmer and bubble for about 20 minutes, stirring occasionally, until it's reduced by about a third. In a small bowl, combine the cornstarch with the water. Drizzle the mixture into the jam mixture, stirring constantly. Boil for 1 minute, until the mixture has thickened. Remove the pan from the heat, and stir in the angostura bitters to combine. Cool the mixture completely.

For the crust, let's make the hand pies. Working with one disc at a time, roll out the dough into a ¼-inch (6-mm) thickness. Cut the dough into 5 rounds, using a 5-inch (13-cm) round cookie cutter. Or, you can trace a 5-inch (13-cm) or so diameter bowl or plate with a paring knife to make the rounds. You may need to reroll the dough once to get five rounds. Repeat with the second disc of dough.

Fill a small dish with water and use your finger to moisten the edge of one-half of a round. Add 2 level tablespoons (40 g) of the strawberry filling to one side of the dough, leaving about a ½-inch (1.3-cm) border of dough from the edge. Fold over the dough to create a half-moon, and press the edges firmly together to seal them. Crimp the edges with the tines of a fork. Repeat to make the rest of the hand pies.

Clip a candy thermometer to the side of a large cast-iron Dutch oven or heavy-bottomed pot. Fill it with enough oil to go about 3 inches (8 cm) up the side of the pot. Heat the oil over medium heat until it reaches 375°F (190°C). This will take about 15 minutes or so.

(continued)

STRAWBERRY ANGOSTURA HAND PIES (CONTINUED)

For the glaze, whisk together the powdered sugar, milk and salt in a small bowl and set it aside.

Line a rimmed baking sheet with foil or parchment paper, and place a cooling rack on top. This is where we'll land the pies after frying, so keep it near the pot. When the oil is up to temperature, use a spider or large slotted spoon to gently lower in two hand pies, one at a time. Fry the hand pies on the first side until deep golden brown, about 3 minutes. Note that, if you use the All-Purpose Dough, plant-based variation (page 22), the color won't be quite as dark.

Flip the pies, using the slotted spoon, and fry for 3 minutes, until deep golden brown on that side. Transfer the pies to the prepared rack. Be sure to monitor the temperature of the oil. It's normal for the temperature to fluctuate when adding and removing pies. If it drops in temperature, let it come back up to 375°F (190°C) before frying the next batch. Turn the heat down a bit if the temperature starts to creep above 375°F (190°C). Add the next two pies to the pot, and repeat the process.

While the next batch is frying, use a pastry brush to brush glaze on the tops of the freshly fried hand pies. Repeat the frying and glazing process with the rest of the hand pies. Even if the outside feels cool to the touch, the filling stays lava hot for quite a while, so wait at least 15 to 20 minutes before serving the pies.

THINK SCRAPPY! Have some leftover dough scraps? Put them to good use with a recipe from the Waste Not, Want Not chapter (page 181).

PIZZA-VIBE HAND PIES WITH SALAMI, FENNEL AND FONTINA

If I could pick only one savory hand pie, it'd be these. The combination of salty salami, the peppery, licoricey bite of fennel and creamy, nutty fontina cheese is crazy good. The juicy crushed tomatoes running throughout means these pies self-sauce, so no need for extra dip on the side. And the hints of dried oregano and granulated garlic baked right into the golden tops give definite old-school pizzeria vibes. These are a super fun and tasty dinner when you want the pizza experience without the delivery charge.

YIELD
Makes 10 (6-inch [15-cm]) hand pies

INGREDIENTS
· 1¼ cups (325 g) crushed, canned tomatoes, drained

· 1 tbsp (15 ml) olive oil

· 1 medium bulb (140 g) fennel, cut into ¼-inch (6-mm) cubes

· 3 cloves garlic, roughly chopped

· Salt

· Freshly ground black pepper

· 7 oz (198 g) fontina cheese, cut into ¼-inch (6-mm) cubes (see tip)

· 5 oz (140 g) sopressata salami, cut into ¼-inch (6-mm) cubes

· 1 tsp dried oregano

· ½ tsp crushed red pepper

· 1 tsp crushed fennel seeds

· 1 recipe All-Purpose Dough (page 22), patted into two discs

· 1 egg, lightly beaten

· Flaky salt

· 1 tsp granulated garlic

· 2 tsp dried oregano

DIRECTIONS

Set a large fine-mesh strainer over a large bowl, and add the can of crushed tomatoes. Allow the excess water to drain from the tomatoes while you prepare the rest of the ingredients. Heat a large skillet over medium-low heat. Add the olive oil, fennel and garlic. Season with salt and pepper, and sauté for 5 to 7 minutes, until the fennel is soft and translucent, stirring occasionally. Transfer the mixture to a large bowl. Add the tomatoes to the bowl with the fennel mixture along with the fontina, salami, oregano, crushed red pepper and fennel seeds. Season lightly with salt and pepper, mix well to combine and set aside.

Line a rimmed baking sheet with parchment paper. Working with one disc of dough at a time, roll it out into a ¼-inch (6-mm) thickness. With a 6-inch (15-cm) round cookie cutter, cut 5 rounds, rerolling once, if necessary, to get 5 rounds. You can also trace a 6-inch (15-cm) diameter bowl or plate with a paring knife to make the rounds. Repeat with the second disc of dough. Fill a small dish with water and, working with one round at a time, dip your finger in the water and moisten the edge of half of the round. Spoon about ⅓ cup (85 g) of the filling on one half of the disc, leaving about ½ inch (1.3 cm) of dough from the edge. Fold over the dough to create a half-moon, and press the edges firmly together to seal. Crimp the edges with the tines of a fork or, for an empanada-style presentation, twist the edges of the dough onto itself, sealing as you go. Repeat with the rest of the hand pies. Arrange the hand pies on the prepared baking sheet, leaving about an inch (2.5 cm) between them. Freeze the hand pies for 30 minutes.

Meanwhile, preheat the oven to 350°F (177°C). Brush the hand pies with the beaten egg, then cut a few steam vent holes on the top. Sprinkle each with the flaky salt, granulated garlic and oregano. Bake the pies for 35 to 40 minutes, until deep golden brown. Allow the pies to cool for a few minutes before serving. *See image on page 136.

HOT TIP: Toss the hunk of fontina cheese into the freezer for 10 to 15 minutes before chopping. This makes it easier to cut.

HAVARTI DILL TARTLETS WITH SMOKED SALMON

These little tarts are a sort of hybrid between buckwheat blini with smoked salmon and dill and a really good bagel situation. The creamy, buttery Havarti cheese is a perfect match for the earthy buckwheat crust and salty, briny salmon. As a close friend to salmon, a little fresh dill is always a welcome addition. These are an anytime sort of snack and make a festive brunch, tasty dinner or even a fun appetizer.

YIELD
Makes 6 (4-inch [10-cm]) tarts

INGREDIENTS
· 1 recipe Buckwheat Dough (page 29), patted into one large rectangle

· 1 cup (240 ml) crème fraîche, room temperature

· 1 large egg, room temperature

· Zest of 1 lemon, finely grated

· ½ tsp sea salt

· ½ tsp freshly ground black pepper, plus more for sprinkling on top

· 1 tbsp (3 g) roughly chopped fresh dill, plus more for sprinkling on top

· 6 oz (170 g) Havarti cheese, grated

· 3 oz (84 g) smoked salmon

· Citrusy Whipped Yogurt (page 176), for serving, optional

THINK SCRAPPY! Have some leftover dough scraps? Put them to good use with a recipe from the Waste Not, Want Not chapter (page 181).

DIRECTIONS

Preheat the oven to 375°F (190°C), and line a rimmed baking sheet with parchment paper. On a well-floured surface, roll the dough out into a ¼-inch (6-mm) thick rough rectangle shape. Use a 4-inch (10-cm) round tart pan with a removable bottom to trace six circles with a paring knife, cutting each about an inch (2.5 cm) larger than the circumference of the tart pan. Drape the dough down the side of each pan so as to not stretch out the dough. Using your thumb, trim away the excess dough by gently pressing the dough against the scalloped edge of the pan. Prick all over the bottom and sides of each tart gently with the tines of a fork. Arrange the tarts on the prepared baking sheet, and place it in the freezer for about 30 minutes, until the shells are very firm.

Cut pieces of parchment paper large enough to fit inside the shells and up the sides, with some overhang. Crumple up the parchment a few times to soften it. Smooth it out and fit it inside the shells. Fill up to the top of the shells with pie weights, dried beans or rice. Bake the shells for 20 minutes, until the dough is set. Remove the weights and the parchment. Bake for 5 minutes or so, until the dough has just gone from shiny to matte. Reduce the oven temperature to 350°F (177°C).

Meanwhile, make the filling while the shells bake. In a bowl, whisk together the crème fraîche, egg, lemon zest, salt, pepper and dill.

Sprinkle 1 ounce (28 g) of Havarti in the bottom of each tart. Divide the filling evenly among the tarts, spooning it over the cheese. Bake the tarts for 25 to 30 minutes, until the filling is set, firm and golden in spots. When the tart molds are cool enough to handle, remove the tarts from the molds and transfer them to plates or a serving platter.

Top each tart with ½ ounce (14 g) of the salmon, a few generous grinds of black pepper, a sprinkling of fresh dill and a dollop of the yogurt, if you'd like.

CHERRY LIME HAND PIES

Cherry limeade will always remind me of a family road trip we took one summer. We were in the middle of nowhere, and everyone was tired, hungry and cranky. Then, out of thin air it seemed, a Sonic Drive-In appeared. I ordered an enormous cherry limeade, and I don't think anything has ever quenched my thirst to this day quite like that limeade did. With that irresistible tart and sweet combination in mind, I created a filling that captures the same balance and made these little hand pies. The rich, fresh and sweet summer cherries and zing of exotic lime really are magic together.

YIELD
Makes 8 (4-inch [10-cm]) hand pies

INGREDIENTS
· 2 cups (343 g) roughly chopped fresh cherries

· ½ cup (100 g) granulated sugar

· 1 tsp cream of tartar

· Pinch of sea salt

· 2 tbsp (30 ml) freshly squeezed lime juice

· 1 tbsp (9 g) cornstarch

· 1 tbsp (15 ml) water

· Zest of 2 limes, finely grated

· 1 recipe All-Purpose Dough (page 22), patted into 1 large disc

· 1 egg, lightly beaten

· Demerara sugar

DIRECTIONS
In a medium saucepan over medium heat, cook the cherries, granulated sugar, cream of tartar, salt and lime juice, stirring occasionally and letting the mixture bubble until the cherries have softened and the juices have thickened slightly, about 15 minutes. Mix the cornstarch with the water in a small bowl, then stir it into the cherry mixture. Let it boil for about a minute or so, until the juices have thickened. Remove the pan from the heat, and stir in the lime zest. Allow the filling to cool completely.

Line two rimmed baking sheets with parchment paper. On a well-floured work surface, roll the dough out to about ⅛ inch (3 mm) thick. Use a 4-inch (10-cm) biscuit or round cookie cutter to cut out 16 discs, rerolling the scraps as necessary. Working with one hand pie at a time, brush the edges of one disc with the beaten egg. Spoon about 2 tablespoons (30 g) of the filling into the center, and top it with another disc, pressing the edges together to seal. Use a fork to crimp the edges to seal. Alternatively, if you'd like to create a lattice top, cut out ½-inch (1.3-cm) wide strips from the scraps slightly longer than the length of the discs. Place strips across the filling, keeping them close together. Now weave strips going the opposite direction by pulling back every other strip and placing another strip on top. Fold back the opposite strips you pulled back last time and place another on top. Repeat with the rest. Use your fingers to press the outer edges of the dough together firmly. Place the round cookie cutter over the hand pie and cut all the excess dough from making the lattice top.

Place the hand pies on the prepared baking sheets about 1 inch (2.5 cm) apart. Freeze the hand pies for 30 minutes, or until firm.

Meanwhile, preheat the oven to 350°F (177°C). Brush the hand pies with the beaten egg, sprinkle them with the demerara sugar and cut a few vent holes on top (unless they're lattice-topped). Bake them for 30 to 35 minutes, until the crusts are deep golden brown and puffed. Allow them to cool for a few minutes before serving.

BLACKBERRY THYME TURNOVERS

I often pair fruit desserts with herbs for an unexpected savory edge. Blackberries and thyme are a favorite combination. The balance of sweet, summer blackberries, a hint of lemon and earthy thyme make these simple little pies a perfect treat to whip up for unexpected guests or a last-minute snack.

YIELD
Makes 8 (6-inch [15-cm]) turnovers

INGREDIENTS
- 1 lb (454 g) fresh blackberries, washed and patted dry
- ½ cup (100 g) granulated sugar
- Zest of 1 lemon, finely grated
- 2 tbsp (6 g) finely chopped fresh thyme leaves
- 1 tsp vanilla bean paste
- Pinch of sea salt
- 2 tbsp (18 g) cornstarch
- 1 recipe All-Purpose Dough (page 22), patted into two rectangles
- 1 egg, lightly beaten
- Demerara sugar

DIRECTIONS

In a large bowl, combine the blackberries, granulated sugar, lemon zest, thyme, vanilla bean paste and salt, and toss to combine. Sprinkle in the cornstarch, and toss again. Set aside the bowl.

On a well-floured work surface, roll the dough out to a ¼- to ⅛-inch (6- to 3-mm) thick, 12½ x 12½–inch (32 x 32–cm) rectangle. Trim down to 12 x 12 inches (30 x 30 cm) so you have clean, straight edges. Cut the dough into four 6 x 6–inch (15 x 15–cm) squares. Repeat with the second rectangle of dough.

Line a rimmed baking sheet with parchment paper.

To assemble the turnovers, position a square of dough in front of you like a diamond, with points on the top and bottom. Brush the edges of the top two sides of the diamond with the beaten egg. Spoon about ¼ cup (60 g) of the filling into the center, then fold up the other side of the dough over the filling so that both points of the diamond meet. Press the sides together to adhere with the egg wash. Crimp the edges with a fork. Transfer the turnover to the prepared baking sheet. Repeat to make eight turnovers in all. Freeze the pan of turnovers for 30 minutes, or until firm.

Meanwhile, preheat the oven to 350°F (177°C). Brush the tops of the turnovers with beaten egg, cut a few vent holes on top and sprinkle them with the demerara sugar. Bake for 30 to 35 minutes, until the turnovers are puffed and deep-golden brown. Serve on their own or with a scoop of ice cream.

VARIATION: Try this recipe with All-Purpose Dough, herb variation (page 22) with thyme.

ROASTED BEET, WALNUT AND GOAT CHEESE HAND PIES WITH ZA'ATAR

Sweet and earthy beets roasted to tender perfection, the soft crunch of walnuts and creamy, tangy goat cheese are some of my absolute favorite salad toppings. They pair equally beautifully together as a hand pie filling. The bit of earthy, minty and nutty za'atar, a Middle-Eastern spice mix, really makes these little parcels something special and unique. Any leftover beets are great tossed over a salad.

YIELD
Makes 10 (6-inch [15-cm]) hand pies

INGREDIENTS
· 2¼ cups (285 g) beets, peeled and cut into ¼-inch (6-mm) cubes
· 2 tsp (10 ml) olive oil
· ½ tsp plus a pinch of sea salt, divided
· ¼ tsp freshly ground black pepper
· ¾ cup (95 g) walnuts, toasted and cooled
· Zest of 1 large lemon, finely grated
· 2 tsp (5 g) za'atar, plus more for sprinkling on top
· 1 recipe All-Purpose Dough (page 22), patted into two discs
· 8 oz (227 g) chèvre goat cheese, crumbled
· 1 egg, lightly beaten
· Flaky salt

VARIATION: Try this recipe with Buttermilk Dough (page 24).

DIRECTIONS
Preheat the oven to 400°F (204°C). In a large bowl, combine the beets, olive oil, ½ teaspoon of the salt and pepper; toss to coat. Transfer the mixture to a rimmed baking sheet, and spread it into a single layer. Roast for 20 to 25 minutes, until the beets are tender. Transfer the beets back to the bowl you used for tossing them, and set them aside to cool.

Meanwhile, pulse the walnuts and pinch of salt a few times in a food processor, until the mixture resembles coarse crumbs. Add the lemon zest and za'atar, and pulse again to combine. Transfer the mixture to a bowl and set it aside.

Line a rimmed baking sheet with parchment paper.

Working with one disc of dough at a time, roll it out into a ¼-inch (6-mm) thickness. With a 6-inch (15-cm) round cookie cutter, cut the dough into five rounds; you may need to reroll the dough once. If you don't have a cookie cutter that size, trace a bowl or plate about that diameter with a paring knife to make the rounds. Repeat with the second disc of dough.

Fill a small bowl with water. Working with one round at a time, dip your finger in the water to moisten the edge of half the round. Add about 1 tablespoon (8 g) of walnut mixture to one half of the disc, leaving about ½ inch (1.3 cm) of dough at the edge. Add about 2 rounded tablespoons (20 g) of beets and 1 tablespoon (17 g) of goat cheese on top. Fold over the dough to create a half-moon, and press the edges firmly together to seal. Crimp the edges with the tines of a fork or, for an empanada-style presentation, twist the edges of the dough onto itself, sealing as you go. Repeat to make the remaining hand pies. Arrange the hand pies on the prepared baking sheet, leaving about an inch (2.5 cm) between each. Freeze the hand pies for 30 minutes.

Meanwhile, preheat the oven to 350°F (177°C). Brush the hand pies with the beaten egg, then cut a few steam vent holes on the top. Sprinkle each with flaky salt and za'atar. Bake the pies for 35 to 40 minutes, until deep golden brown.

ROSY PEACH GALETTES

My favorite stone fruit in all the land is by far the peach. I wait each year for my local grocery store to get in the season's best freestone peaches during their Peach-O-Rama celebration, and then proceed to load up as many as will fit into a huge paper bag. It hardly seems right to bake with them when they taste so incredible fresh, but if I can manage to part with a few, these little galettes are worth the sacrifice. The sweet and fragrant peaches pair beautifully with just the tiniest whisper of floral rose water, and the hazelnut crust adds a lovely texture and crunch.

YIELD
Makes 6 (4-inch [10-cm]) galettes

INGREDIENTS

· 1 lb (454 g) yellow peaches, freestone if you can find them, cut into ¼-inch (6-mm) slices

· ½ cup (100 g) granulated sugar

· 1 tsp vanilla bean paste

· ½ tsp rose water

· Big pinch of sea salt

· 2 tbsp (18 g) cornstarch

· 1 recipe Any-Nut Dough (page 27), using hazelnuts, patted into six mini discs

· 1 egg, lightly beaten

· Demerara sugar

· Dried rose petals, culinary grade, for serving, optional

· Honey Whipped Cream (page 175) or ice cream, for serving

DIRECTIONS

In a large bowl, toss to combine the peaches, granulated sugar, vanilla bean paste, rose water, salt and cornstarch. Set aside the mixture.

Line a rimmed baking sheet with parchment paper. On a well-floured surface, roll each disc out into a ⅛-inch (3-mm) thick roundish shape about 6 inches (15 cm) in diameter. Divide the filling up evenly among the 6 rounds, mounding the peaches up in the center and leaving about a 2-inch (5-cm) border along the edges. Fold up the dough around the peaches, and transfer the galettes to the prepared baking sheet. Freeze the galettes for 30 minutes.

Meanwhile, preheat the oven to 400°F (204°C). Brush the sides of the dough with the beaten egg, and sprinkle them with the demerara sugar. Bake the galettes for 35 to 40 minutes, until the crust is deep-golden brown. Sprinkle the galettes with a few of the rose petals, if using. Serve them with the Honey Whipped Cream or ice cream.

KALE, PINE NUT AND GOLDEN RAISIN GALETTES

Kale is one of those you-love-it or you-hate-it things. For me, it's my all-time favorite green. These little galettes have all the things I love in a kale salad: the bracing bite of tangy vinegar, salty, umami Parmigiano-Reggiano, crunchy and rich pine nuts and sweet golden raisins to balance out the earthy kale. Bonus: the kale on top crisps as it bakes, making an almost kale-chip texture on top. These little galettes may seem unassuming, but I'd be willing to bet they'll turn even the biggest skeptic into an emphatic kale lover.

YIELD
Makes 6 (4-inch [10-cm]) galettes

INGREDIENTS
· 1 tbsp (15 ml) olive oil

· 2 large cloves garlic, finely chopped

· 1 large bunch (120 g) lacinato kale, stems removed and roughly chopped

· 1 tbsp (15 ml) apple cider vinegar

· ¼ cup (50 g) golden raisins, roughly chopped

· ⅓ cup (45 g) pine nuts, toasted

· ¼ cup plus 2 tbsp (57 g) finely grated Parmigiano-Reggiano

· Zest of 1 medium lemon, finely grated

· ½ tsp sea salt

· ½ tsp freshly ground black pepper

· 1 recipe Rye Dough (page 26), patted into six mini discs

· 1 egg, lightly beaten

· Flaky salt

DIRECTIONS
Heat the olive oil in a large skillet over medium heat, then add the garlic. Sauté it for about 30 seconds, just until fragrant, then add the kale. Sauté for a minute or two, just until it starts to soften. Drizzle in the vinegar, and toss again to combine. Once the vinegar has evaporated, shut off the heat and transfer the kale to a large bowl. Add the raisins, pine nuts, Parmigiano, lemon zest, salt and pepper. Stir to combine, and set aside the bowl.

Line a rimmed baking sheet with parchment paper. On a well-floured surface, roll each disc out into a ⅛-inch (3-mm) thick roundish shape about 6 inches (15 cm) in diameter. Divide the filling evenly among the 6 rounds, leaving about a 2-inch (5-cm) border along the edges. The raisins and pine nuts will have a tendency to fall to the bottom of the bowl, so be sure to distribute them evenly among the galettes. Fold up the dough around the filling and transfer the galettes to the prepared baking sheet. Freeze the galettes for 30 minutes.

Meanwhile, preheat the oven to 400°F (204°C). Brush the sides of the galettes with the beaten egg, then sprinkle them with the flaky salt. Bake the galettes for 35 to 40 minutes, until the crust is deep golden brown. Serve warm.

RASPBERRY CHEESECAKE BLOSSOMS

There's something about a tangy raspberry and vanilla-speckled cheesecake filling in a buttery, flaky package that's just inherently delicious. Not unlike a cheese Danish, these are a fast-track way of having your cheesecake and eating it too, in a lot less time than it would take to make an actual cheesecake. These are tasty warm from the oven or even room temperature the next day.

YIELD

Makes 8 (4-inch [10-cm]) blossoms

INGREDIENTS

· 4 oz (113 g) full-fat cream cheese, room temperature

· ½ cup (63 g) powdered sugar, plus more for serving

· 1 large egg yolk, room temperature

· 2 tsp (10 ml) vanilla bean paste

· Big pinch of sea salt

· 2 cups (274 g) fresh raspberries, washed and patted dry

· 2 tbsp (13 g) granulated sugar

· 1 tbsp (9 g) cornstarch

· 1 tsp freshly squeezed lemon juice

· 1 recipe All-Purpose Dough (page 22), patted into 2 rectangles

· 1 egg, lightly beaten

DIRECTIONS

In a medium bowl, combine the cream cheese, powdered sugar, egg yolk, vanilla bean paste and salt, and beat the mixture with a hand mixer until smooth. Set aside. In another bowl, combine the raspberries, granulated sugar, cornstarch and lemon juice, and toss to combine, being careful not to break up the raspberries too much. Set aside.

Line a rimmed baking sheet with parchment paper. On a well-floured surface, roll out one of the rectangles of dough into a 10 x 10–inch (25 x 25–cm) square, trimming any rough edges. Cut the square into 4 squares, each 5 x 5 inches (13 x 13 cm). Repeat with the second rectangle of dough so that you have 8 squares total.

Spoon a rounded tablespoon (30 g) of the cheesecake filling onto the center of each square, then spread it out into an even circle, leaving about 1 inch (2.5 cm) of dough around all sides. Top the cheesecake mixture with about a tablespoon (38 g) of the raspberry mixture. Fold up the dough in the center of each side, pinching the sides toward the center to make a petal shape. Repeat to make the rest of the blossoms, then place them on the prepared baking sheet, spacing them about an inch (2.5 cm) apart. Freeze the blossoms for 30 minutes.

Meanwhile, preheat the oven to 400°F (204°C). Brush the sides of the dough with the beaten egg. Bake the blossoms for 30 to 35 minutes, until the crust is deep golden brown. Dust them with the powdered sugar. Serve warm or room temperature.

SWEDISH CARDAMOM ROLL HAND PIES

A few years ago, I stumbled upon and fell in love with the concept of Fika, the Swedish way of taking a little break sometime during the day to enjoy coffee and a sweet treat. It's an opportunity to slow down for a moment and simply enjoy life. Lovely, right? Perhaps one of the most iconic Swedish sweets is kardemummabullar, *or cardamom rolls: rich, sweet rolls filled with fragrant cardamom and topped with crunchy pearl sugar. These little pastries have all the wonderful flavors of those rolls in portable pie form, with a few little twists. Personally, I think we should adopt Fika in the States. Consider this recipe my contribution toward the movement.*

YIELD
Makes 12 (3-inch [8-cm]) hand pies

INGREDIENTS
· ¼ cup (56 g) unsalted butter, room temperature
· ¾ cup (195 g) light brown sugar, packed
· 1 tbsp (5 g) ground cardamom
· Zest of 1 large orange, finely grated
· 3 tbsp (24 g) all-purpose flour
· Pinch of sea salt
· 1 recipe All-Purpose Dough (page 22), patted into two discs
· 1 large egg, beaten
· 2 tbsp (24 g) Swedish pearl sugar (see tip)

HOT TIP: If you can't find Swedish pearl sugar, though it is pretty and fun, these will be equally delicious sprinkled with turbinado or demerara sugar.

DIRECTIONS
In a medium bowl, stir together the butter, brown sugar, cardamom, orange zest, flour and salt, until the mixture is smooth and well combined. Set it aside.

Line a rimmed baking sheet with parchment paper. Work with only one disc of dough at a time and leave the other in the fridge. On a lightly floured work surface, roll the dough out ⅛ inch (3 mm) thick. Using a 3-inch (8-cm) round cookie or biscuit cutter, cut out 12 rounds, re-rolling the dough once if necessary. Transfer the rounds to the prepared baking sheet in a single layer and refrigerate them while you roll out the top layer. Repeat the rolling and cutting process with the second disc of dough.

Pull the bases out of the fridge and, working with one hand pie at a time, brush the base all over with the beaten egg. Spoon 1 level tablespoon (15 g) of filling onto the center, flattening it out slightly into a disc and leaving about ½ inch (1.3 cm) around all sides. Place a round of dough on top and use your fingers to seal the edges together around the whole hand pie. Dip the tines of a fork in flour and press all around the edges of the hand pie to seal it. Repeat to make the rest of the hand pies, then place them all back on the baking sheet and freeze them for 30 minutes.

Meanwhile, preheat the oven to 350°F (177°C). After the 30 minutes of chilling, brush each pie with egg wash, cut four small ventholes in the tops with a paring knife and sprinkle them with the pearl sugar. Since the pies are frozen solid, it's best to work on one at a time, otherwise the egg wash freezes too quickly for the pearl sugar to adhere. Bake the pies for 30 to 35 minutes, until golden brown. Cool the pies before serving.

THINK SCRAPPY! Have some leftover dough scraps? Put them to good use with a recipe from the Waste Not, Want Not chapter (page 181).

CHIPOTLE VEGETABLE CHILI MINI POT PIES

Growing up, my mom always had chili and cornbread in the dinner rotation, especially during the colder winter months. While I did enjoy the chili, slathering a fat piece of cornbread with soft butter and a healthy drizzle of honey was always my favorite part. These impossibly adorable mini chili pot pies are chili and cornbread all in one, with smoky spices and tons of veggies all topped with a crispy cornmeal crust lid. Top them just as you would your favorite bowl of chili and they make for a perfect, cozy dinner.

YIELD
Makes 8 (1-cup [240-ml]) mini pot pies

INGREDIENTS
Chili
- 2 tbsp (30 ml) avocado oil
- 1 large white or yellow onion, roughly chopped
- 2 large sweet red, yellow or orange bell peppers, roughly chopped
- 4 cloves garlic, finely chopped
- Sea salt
- 2 tsp (3 g) smoked paprika
- 1 tsp dried oregano
- 2 tbsp (40 g) tomato paste
- 2 chipotle peppers from a (7-oz [200-g]) can of chipotle peppers in adobo sauce, finely chopped
- 1 tbsp (15 g) adobo sauce, reserved from can
- 1 (15-oz [425-g]) can pinto beans, drained and rinsed
- 1 (28-oz [794-g]) can diced tomatoes
- 2 tsp (10 ml) honey
- 1 cup (240 ml) vegetable stock

Crust
- 1 recipe Cornmeal Dough (page 28), patted into a large disc
- 1 egg, lightly beaten
- Flaky salt

For Serving
- Sour cream
- Cilantro
- Red onion, roughly chopped, or scallions

DIRECTIONS

In a large heavy-bottomed pot, heat the oil over medium heat. Add the onion, bell peppers and garlic; season with salt. Sauté for a few minutes, stirring occasionally and letting the vegetables sweat. Sprinkle in the paprika and oregano and stir to incorporate, letting the spices bloom in the oil for about a minute or so. Add the tomato paste, chipotle peppers and adobo sauce, and stir to coat the vegetables. Let the mixture cook for another minute or so. Add the beans, tomatoes, honey and vegetable stock. Stir everything to combine it. Bring the chili to a simmer, then reduce the heat to medium-low and cook for 30 minutes or so, until the liquid has reduced and the chili has thickened. Remove the pan from the heat and set it aside.

Preheat the oven to 400°F (204°C), and line a rimmed baking sheet with foil. On a well-floured surface, roll the dough out to about ¼-inch (6-mm) thickness, and use a 1-cup (240-ml) ramekin to trace a circle in the dough. Repeat with the rest of the dough so you have eight circles. Fill each ramekin with chili, leaving about ¼-inch (6-mm) of space at the top. Place the ramekins on the foil-lined sheet, and top each with the circles of dough, pressing them into the ramekin so they're snug against the filling. Brush with the beaten egg, and sprinkle with the flaky salt.

Bake the pot pies for 25 to 30 minutes, until the crust has puffed and is a deep golden brown. To serve, top with a dollop of sour cream and a sprinkling of cilantro and red onion.

'NDUJA, SMOKED MOZZARELLA AND BROCCOLINI HAND PIES

These ultrasavory little hand pies are cozy Italian comfort flavors all bundled in a convenient little package. If you've never had 'nduja, a spicy, spreadable sausage, it is a real treat. The richness and spice combined with the smoky, milky mozzarella and the crisp and fresh bite of the green broccolini make these a complete meal in a tiny package.

YIELD

Makes 12 (3 x 4½–inch [8 x 11–cm]) hand pies

INGREDIENTS

· 1 tbsp (15 ml) olive oil

· 6 oz (170 g) broccolini, cut into ½-inch (1.3-cm) pieces

· Freshly ground black pepper

· 2 large cloves garlic, finely chopped

· 1 recipe Rye Dough (page 26), patted into two rectangles

· 6 oz (170 g) 'nduja (see tip)

· 6 oz (170 g) smoked mozzarella cheese, cut into ¼-inch (6-mm) slices

· 1 egg, lightly beaten

· Flaky salt

DIRECTIONS

Heat a large skillet over medium heat, and add the olive oil. Once the oil is warm, add the broccolini. Season with pepper. Sauté, stirring occasionally, until the broccolini is crisp-tender, 7 to 9 minutes. Add the garlic and sauté another minute, just until fragrant. Remove the broccolini from the heat, and set it aside to cool.

Line a rimmed baking sheet with parchment paper. On a well-floured surface, roll one of the rectangles of dough out into an ⅛-inch (3-mm) thick rectangle, 12 x 13½ inches (30 x 34 cm). Cut the dough into 12 rectangles, each 3 x 4½ inches (8 x 11 cm), and place them on the prepared baking sheet, about an inch (2.5 cm) apart. Refrigerate the squares while you repeat with the second rectangle of dough.

Pull the bottoms out of the fridge, and spread ½ ounce (14 g) of 'nduja onto each rectangle, leaving about a ½-inch (1.3-cm) border along all sides. Top each with ½ ounce (14 g) of broccolini (about a tablespoon), followed by a ½-ounce (14 g) slice of mozzarella, trimming it to size, if necessary, to fit on top of the broccolini mixture. Brush the edges with the beaten egg and top each with the remaining rectangles, pressing the edges together and crimping them with a fork to seal. Place the baking sheet in the freezer for 30 minutes.

Meanwhile, preheat the oven to 350°F (177°C). Brush each hand pie with the beaten egg, cut a few vent holes and sprinkle the crust with the flaky salt. Bake for 30 to 35 minutes, until golden brown. Serve warm.

HOT TIP: You can find 'nduja at most specialty grocery stores in the cured meats section or online. It can sometimes be a bit tricky to find, but trust me, it's well worth seeking out. A great brand to look for is La Quercia; it's made with high-quality ingredients and is pretty widely available.

LIL' SMOKY SAUSAGE ROLLS WITH HOT AND SWEET MUSTARD

Hands down the most exciting dinner my mom would make us growing up were what we called lil' smokies: little smoked cocktail sausages rolled up in crescent dough from the can with a slice of cheddar cheese and, of course, plenty of ketchup and mustard for dipping. It was a rare occasion and special treat when she did make them, probably due to the complete lack of nutritional value they offered; I suppose that added to the appeal. We even used to fight over the ones with the biggest cheese skirts, the little bits of cheddar that oozed out during baking and created a cheese crisp. These are an updated and elevated version of my childhood favorite. Serve them as a tasty appetizer for game night or as a fun dinner.

YIELD
Makes 12 sausage rolls

INGREDIENTS
· 1 recipe All-Purpose Dough (page 22), patted into one large rectangle

· 2 oz (54 g) extra sharp cheddar cheese, shredded

· 1 egg, lightly beaten

· 1 (12-oz [340-g]) package smoked sausages, fully cooked

· Poppy or sesame seeds or a combination

· ¼ cup (70 g) Dijon mustard

· 2 tbsp (30 g) whole-grain mustard

· 2 tsp (10 ml) honey

DIRECTIONS

Line a rimmed baking sheet with parchment paper. On a well-floured work surface, roll out the dough into a ¼-inch (6-mm) thick rectangle. Trim it down to 6 inches (15 cm) long by 20 inches (51 cm) wide. Make tick-marks with a paring knife every 5 inches (13 cm) along the 20-inch (51-cm) side. Use a ruler to cut along the tick marks so that you end up with four 5 x 6–inch (13 x 15–cm) rectangles. With the shorter side facing you, sprinkle ½ ounce (14 g) of cheese in the center of each piece, leaving about 2 inches (5 cm) of dough on either side. Brush one edge with the beaten egg. Place the sausage on the opposite end of the egg wash, and roll the dough up around the sausage, like a cinnamon roll. Gently press the egg-washed end onto the dough to seal. Place the sausage roll on the prepared baking sheet, seam side down. Repeat with the rest of the sausages. Freeze the sausage rolls for 30 minutes.

Meanwhile, preheat the oven to 400°F (204°C). Slice each sausage into 3 equal pieces, 1½ to 2 inches (4 to 5 cm) long, and arrange them on the baking sheet about an inch (2.5 cm) apart. Brush the rolls with egg wash, and sprinkle with the poppy or sesame seeds. Bake the rolls for 25 to 30 minutes, until they are puffed and deep golden brown. Allow the rolls to cool for a few minutes before serving.

To make the hot and sweet mustard, mix the Dijon mustard, whole-grain mustard and honey in a small bowl, and set it aside until ready to serve.

VARIATION: Try this recipe with Cheddar Dough (page 25).

THINK SCRAPPY! Have some leftover dough scraps? Put them to good use with a recipe from the Waste Not, Want Not chapter (page 181).

SALTY PRETZEL HAZELNUT AND CARAMEL BANANA CREAM TARTS

These little tartlets are for all the banana lovers out there. I set out to create a version of banana cream pie that wasn't so texturally one-note. The crispy, salty pretzel crust is the perfect vehicle to deliver the fluffy caramel-swirled whipped cream and fresh banana slices. Don't forget the sneaky smear of Nutella® on the bottom.

YIELD
Makes 6 (4-inch [10-cm]) tarts

INGREDIENTS
Crust
- 6 oz (170 g) salted pretzels
- 4 oz (113 g) roasted hazelnuts
- ¼ cup (60 ml) honey
- 6 tbsp (84 g) unsalted butter, melted and cooled
- Pinch of sea salt, optional

Filling
- 6 tbsp (111 g) chocolate hazelnut spread, such as Nutella
- 2 cups (480 ml) heavy whipping cream, cold
- ½ cup (120 ml) Salted Clementine Caramel Sauce (page 179)
- 3 medium bananas
- 2 tbsp (17 g) roasted hazelnuts, roughly chopped

DIRECTIONS
For the crust, preheat the oven to 350°F (177°C), and line a rimmed baking sheet with foil. In a food processor, process the pretzels and hazelnuts into fine crumbs. Transfer them to a medium bowl, add the honey and butter and stir to combine. Depending on how salty your pretzels are, you may need to add a pinch of salt, so give the crust a taste and add a pinch if necessary, keeping in mind the filling is quite sweet, so a bit of salt is nice to balance everything out. Divide the crust evenly among six 4-inch (10-cm) round tart pans with removable bottoms, and press the dough into the sides and bottom, using the bottom of a glass or measuring cup to help you press it in. Place the tarts on the prepared baking sheet. Bake the crusts for 15 to 20 minutes, until firm and crisp. Cool the crusts completely.

For the filling, spread a tablespoon (19 g) of the chocolate hazelnut spread evenly in the bottom of each tart.

Whip the heavy cream to soft peaks. Fold in the caramel sauce, and divide the whipped cream mixture evenly among the tart shells. Cut the bananas in half, then slice each half lengthwise into three slices. Nestle three slices on top of each tart, side by side. Sprinkle the hazelnuts on top. Serve the tarts immediately.

> HOT TIP: To make prep the day of serving these tarts simpler, make the Salted Clementine Caramel Sauce a day in advance, and keep it on the counter at room temperature. That way, it's nice and firm when you're ready to assemble the tarts.

FRIENDS OF PIE

While each recipe in this book could really stand on its own, sometimes a pie just needs a friend. These recipes are the perfect complement for your slice for such occasions where whipped cream is simply a necessity, a dollop of tangy yogurt cuts through a rich slice or a drizzle of caramel rounds out the perfect bite.

HONEY WHIPPED CREAM

I prefer the delicate, floral sweetness of honey to the usual granulated or powdered sugar in whipped cream. This is a versatile topping for just about any sweet pie in the book and beyond.

YIELD
Makes about 4 cups (960 ml)

INGREDIENTS
· 16 oz (473 ml) heavy whipping cream, cold
· 2 tbsp (30 ml) good-quality honey
· 1 tsp vanilla bean paste
· Pinch of sea salt

DIRECTIONS
In the bowl of a stand mixer or a large bowl with a hand mixer or with a whisk by hand, whip the cream on high until the whisk starts to leave marks in the surface of the cream but it's not quite at soft peaks yet, about 2 minutes. Add the honey, vanilla bean paste and salt, and continue whipping until soft peaks form and the honey is fully incorporated.

CITRUSY WHIPPED YOGURT

This is like the tangy, savory version of whipped cream. Aerated, fluffy and so perfect for adding a bit of lightness to a rich slice.

YIELD
Makes about 3 cups (720 ml)

INGREDIENTS
· 16 oz (473 ml) full-fat Greek yogurt

· Zest of 1 lemon, finely grated

· ½ tsp sea salt

· ½ cup (120 ml) heavy whipping cream, cold

DIRECTIONS
In a medium bowl, stir to combine the yogurt, lemon zest and salt. In the bowl of a stand mixer fitted with the whisk attachment, in a large bowl with a hand mixer or by hand, beat the heavy cream on high until stiff peaks form, 2 to 3 minutes. Add the whipped cream to the yogurt mixture, and use a rubber spatula to gently fold in the cream, being careful not to deflate the cream.

SALTED CLEMENTINE CARAMEL SAUCE

This surprisingly delightful flavor combination is the caramel sauce you never knew you needed. The sharp acidity of the fragrant clementine cuts through the richness of the would-be-too-sweet caramel and brings balance, complexity and a whole new perspective of what caramel can be. Drizzle it on EVERYTHING. And if you can't find clementines, any sweet orange will do.

YIELD
Makes about 1 cup (240 ml) caramel sauce

INGREDIENTS
· 1 cup (200 g) granulated sugar

· ¼ cup (60 ml) water

· ½ cup (120 ml) freshly squeezed clementine juice, from about 4 to 5 clementines

· ½ cup (112 g) unsalted butter, room temperature, cut into small pieces

· 1 tsp sea salt

· 2 tsp (10 ml) vanilla bean paste

DIRECTIONS
Fill a small bowl with water and have a pastry brush handy and set aside. Combine the sugar and water in a 3- or 4-quart (2.8- or 3.8-L) straight-sided, heavy-bottomed saucepot and swirl the pan gently to saturate all the sugar with the water. Melt the sugar and water over medium heat, swirling the pot gently every so often, but not stirring. Dip the pastry brush in the bowl of water, and brush away from the sides of the pot any sugar granules that haven't melted. This will prevent the caramel from crystallizing. Continue cooking, swirling the pot often, until the sugar is dark amber in color and smells toasty, about 10 minutes.

Remove the pan from the heat and, while whisking constantly, stream in the clementine juice. The sugar will sputter and bubble up quite a bit, and the sugar will momentarily clump up, but don't fret. Place the pot back over the heat and whisk constantly until the mixture comes back together and the sugar clumps dissolve into the clementine juice, 2 to 3 minutes. Cook, continuing to whisk, until the mixture thickens, 3 to 5 minutes. Turn off the heat and whisk in the butter until it's completely melted. Add the salt and vanilla bean paste, and whisk again until smooth. The caramel can be served warm or at room temperature.

WASTE NOT, WANT NOT

Inevitably, when making some pies from this book, you're going to run into a scenario where you'll have some scraps of dough left over. This is not a bad thing, and please, whatever you do, don't throw it out! These ingenious little recipes not only keep those scraps out of the bin, but transform them into something truly tasty, like the Herby Garlic Croutons (page 184) or the Smoky Sesame Cheese Twigs (page 192). Each recipe is designed to be flexible and adaptable to the amount of scraps you're working with, so don't fret too much over being precise. Next time you find yourself with some scraps, flip through these recipes and put them to good use!

ANY CITRUS ZEST PIE CRUST COOKIES

Anytime my mom made a pie, she always let me help roll out the leftover crust scraps. We'd sprinkle them with a bit of sugar, and bake them up into little cookies. These are a slightly fancier version, with the addition of some fragrant citrus zest.

YIELD
Makes 10–20 cookies

INGREDIENTS
· ½ cup (100 g) granulated sugar

· 1 tsp finely grated citrus zest, such as lemon, lime, orange, grapefruit or a mixture

· 4–6 oz (113–170 g) leftover dough, such as All-Purpose (page 22), Buttermilk (page 24), etc.

· 1 egg, lightly beaten

DIRECTIONS
Preheat the oven to 350°F (177°C), and line a rimmed baking sheet with parchment paper.

Put the sugar in a bowl and zest your citrus of choice directly over the sugar, catching all the essential oils. With your fingers, rub the zest into the sugar, releasing all its fragrant essential oils.

On a floured work surface, roll the dough out to about ¼ inch (6 mm) thick and brush it with the egg. Generously sprinkle the dough with the citrus sugar, gently pressing the sugar into the surface of the dough with your fingers. Use a knife to cut irregular shapes or a 1- to 2-inch (2.5- to 5-cm) biscuit cutter. Transfer the cookies to the prepared baking sheet.

Bake the cookies for 15 to 20 minutes, until they are puffed and golden brown. Cool before serving.

HERBY GARLIC CROUTONS

Try whipping up a batch of these next time you serve a big green salad. For an unexpected delight, swap them for your usual run-of-the-mill croutons.

YIELD
Makes about 20 croutons

INGREDIENTS
· 1 tbsp (14 g) unsalted butter

· 2 cloves garlic, finely minced

· 1 tbsp (3 g) mixture of finely chopped fresh herbs, such as chives, rosemary, thyme and sage

· 4–6 oz (113–170 g) leftover dough, such as All-Purpose (page 22), Buttermilk (page 24), Cheddar (page 25), Cornmeal (page 28), etc.

· Sea salt

· Cracked black pepper

DIRECTIONS
Preheat the oven to 350°F (177°C), and line a rimmed baking sheet with parchment paper.

In a small pot over medium heat, combine the butter, garlic and herbs, and melt the butter. Remove the pan from the heat.

On a floured work surface, roll the dough out to a ¼- to ½-inch (6-mm to 1.3-cm) thick rectangle, and brush it generously with the butter mixture. Sprinkle it with the salt and pepper. Cut the dough into ½-inch (1.3-cm) cubes. Spread the cubes evenly on the prepared baking sheet.

Bake the croutons until crisp and deep golden brown, 20 to 25 minutes. Serve on salads, soups or on their own as a snack.

SOLDIERS

These are the perfect little side to dip into soups, or even the soft, drippy yolk of a poached or soft-boiled egg at breakfast time.

YIELD
Makes 3–4 soldiers

INGREDIENTS
· 4–6 oz (113–170 g) leftover dough, such as All-Purpose (page 22), Buttermilk (page 24), Cheddar (page 25), Cornmeal (page 28), etc.

· 1 egg, lightly beaten

· Sea salt

· Cracked black pepper

DIRECTIONS
Preheat the oven to 400°F (204°C), and line a rimmed baking sheet with parchment paper.

On a floured work surface, roll the dough out to a ½-inch (1.3-cm) thick rectangle, and trim the edges so they're straight. Slice the dough into 1-inch (2.5-cm) strips. Place the strips on the prepared baking sheet, brush with the beaten egg, then sprinkle with salt and pepper.

Bake the strips for 20 to 25 minutes, until they are deep golden brown.

SPICY ICE CREAM CRUMBLE

The deep spices here lend themselves well to sweet, creamy ice cream and help to cut through the richness. The buttery crust bakes up into the crispiest crumbles for a nice textural contrast to the ice cream.

YIELD
Makes about 1 cup (74 g)

INGREDIENTS
· 2 tbsp (25 g) demerara sugar

· ¼ tsp freshly ground black pepper

· ¼ tsp ground cardamom

· ¼ tsp ground ginger

· ¼ tsp ground cinnamon

· ⅛ tsp ground cloves

· Pinch of sea salt

· 4–6 oz (113–170 g) leftover dough, such as All-Purpose (page 22) or Buttermilk (page 24)

· 1 egg, lightly beaten

DIRECTIONS
Preheat the oven to 350°F (177°C). In a small bowl, mix together the sugar, pepper, cardamom, ginger, cinnamon, cloves and salt.

On a floured work surface, roll the dough out to about ⅛ inch (3 mm) thick and brush it with the beaten egg. Sprinkle the dough liberally with the sugar and spice mixture.

Bake the dough for 20 to 25 minutes, until it's deep golden brown and very crisp. Allow the crumble to cool, then break it up into small pieces. Sprinkle the pieces all over ice cream. Better yet, drizzle some of the Salted Clementine Caramel Sauce (page 179) on the crumble, too.

CINNAMON SUGAR SPIRALS

These are part pie crust, part cookie, part cinnamon roll and all kinds of delicious. The cinnamon sugar caramelizes on the bottom of the spirals, adding a crispy sugar shell around the flaky crust.

YIELD
Makes 10–15 spiral cookies

INGREDIENTS
· ¼ cup (50 g) granulated sugar

· 1 tsp ground cinnamon

· Pinch of sea salt

· 4–6 oz (113–170 g) leftover dough, such as All-Purpose (page 22) or Buttermilk (page 24)

· 1 egg, lightly beaten

DIRECTIONS
Preheat the oven to 350°F (177°C), and line a rimmed baking sheet with parchment paper.

In a small bowl, mix together the sugar, cinnamon and salt.

On a floured work surface, roll the dough out into a rough rectangle about ⅛ inch (3 mm) thick, about 10 x 6 inches (25 x 15 cm). Trim the edges to make them straight. Brush the entire surface with the egg. Sprinkle the sugar mixture evenly across the entire surface of the dough, except for about ½ inch (1.3 cm) at one of the shorter ends. With the shorter side opposite the egg-washed edge facing you, roll the dough up into a tight log. When you get to the end, seal the bare edge with the egg wash on it, adhering it to the underside of the log. Roll the log so it's seam side down, and freeze it for 15 to 20 minutes, until firm.

Slice the log into ¼-inch (6-mm) thick slices and arrange them on the prepared baking sheet about an inch (2.5 cm) apart.

Bake the spirals for 20 to 25 minutes, until golden brown. The sugar mixture may leak out a bit, but it'll caramelize on the bottom and stay with the cookie. Cool, then serve.

SMOKY SESAME CHEESE TWIGS

These are a fun and low-key snack to put out at a party that feels much fancier than they are. Serve them upright in a glass with a tray of olives, nuts and cheeses, and watch them disappear.

YIELD
Makes 12–15 cheese twigs

INGREDIENTS
· ¾ tsp smoked paprika

· ¼ tsp cayenne

· 1 tsp toasted white sesame seeds

· 4–6 oz (113–170 g) leftover dough such as All-Purpose (page 22), Cheddar (page 25) or Buttermilk (page 24)

· 1 egg, lightly beaten

· ¼ cup (18 g) finely grated hard, salty cheese, such as Parmigiano-Reggiano, pecorino or Grana Padano

DIRECTIONS
Preheat the oven to 350°F (177°C), and line a rimmed baking sheet with parchment paper.

In a small bowl, mix together the paprika, cayenne and sesame seeds.

On a floured work surface, roll the dough out into a rough rectangle about ¼ inch (6 mm) thick, and brush it with the beaten egg. Evenly sprinkle the spice mixture on the dough, followed by the cheese. Press the cheese and spices lightly into the dough with your hands. Cut the dough into ¼-inch (6-mm) thick strips, and transfer them to the prepared baking sheet, spacing the twigs about ½ inch (1.3 cm) apart.

Bake the twigs for 15 to 18 minutes, until very crisp and golden brown. Cool, then serve.

SOURCES

Flourist
Organic all-purpose and rye flours
www.flourist.com

Bob's Red Mill
All-purpose flour, buckwheat flour, rye flour, cornmeal, cornstarch
www.bobsredmill.com

Jacobsen Salt Co.
Kosher sea salt, flaky salt, local honey
www.jacobsensalt.com

Heilala Vanilla
Pure vanilla bean paste
www.heilalavanilla.com

The Spice House
A wonderful resource for just about every whole or ground spice or herb you need
www.thespicehouse.com

India Tree
Natural food coloring, demerara sugar and sparkling sugars
www.indiatree.com

La Quercia Cured Meats
'Nduja and pancetta
www.laquerciashop.com

Dansk
Enamel baking dishes and pots
www.dansk.com

Staub
Cast-iron skillets, Dutch ovens and mini cocottes
www.zwilling.com/us/staub

Nordicware
Half- and quarter-sheet pans
www.nordicware.com

USA Pan
Metal ridged 9-inch (23-cm) pie pans
www.usapan.com

Falcon Enamelware
Enamelware baking sheets, colanders and bowls
www.us.falconenamelware.com

Herriott Grace
Stoneware and porcelain dishes
www.herriottgrace.com

Beau Rush Ceramics
Handmade ceramics
www.beaurushceramics.com

Colleen Hennessey Clayworks
Handmade ceramics
www.colleenhennessey.net

Earthen Shop
Handmade ceramics and home goods
www.earthen-shop.com

Black Swan Handmade
Handmade wooden and copper pie servers
www.blackswanhandmade.com

Hawkins New York
Linen napkins, fine home goods
www.hawkinsnewyork.com

Create and Capture Studios
Handmade and custom photography surfaces and backgrounds
www.createandcapturestudios.com

ACKNOWLEDGMENTS

Mom and Dad, this book may have my name on it, but you gave me the confidence to go out in the world and know I could carve a little piece out for myself, so this book belongs to you, too. I owe it all to you.

Mom, thank you for answering every exhausted phone call, listening to every worry and fear, picking me back up and dusting me off after every meltdown and offering up your kitchen to me. Dad, thank you for making any and every photography background, cutting board and prop I've ever asked for—and we know there's been a lot—and always knowing the answer to "How do you think they made that?" Your endless talent for EVERYTHING still never ceases to amaze me.

Avery, you are the Emile to my Remy. Thank you for being my biggest supporter and for always being as enthusiastic about my wins as I am. I am blessed beyond words to call you sister and best friend. I love you. Evan, thank you for being a spirited supporter of the book from day one!

Mandy, you are the big sister I never had. Thank you for letting me tap your baking knowledge endlessly, for your willingness to indulge me in every unsolicited brainstorming session and for reviewing and critiquing my never-ending string of pecan pie photos. Oh, and for the pot pie recipe. Thank you for always being in my corner. Naynay, Tom, Nanny and Papa: Thank you for loving me and always believing in my dreams.

Holly, thank you—and the girls—for keeping me in the finest eggs, for being my sounding board, always tellin' it like it is and passing out leftover pie tests with me in Pioneer Square on lunch breaks. What an adventure. Your friendship is something I'll always treasure.

Sapana Chandra and Kelsey Siemens, thank you for answering every little question I had about writing a book. You both shared your knowledge and experience so generously, and I only hope I can pay it forward for someone else one day. Megan and Sapana, thank you for being such great sources of support, for your sage advice, encouragement and cheers.

Krystle Jones, Josh Borden, Caitlyn Ishikawa, Laura Scherb, James Hillery, Sarah Licata, Lauren Mitchell, Rylee Foer, Kelly Finn and Kelli Samson: Thank you, not only for testing my recipes tirelessly and with immense enthusiasm, but for being a champion of this book and of me!

To my mighty group of recipe testers, your help has been invaluable in ensuring my recipes made sense and were the best they could be! Kat, Brendan, Erica, Emma, Hannah, Sam and D.J., Kathryn, Annie, Emily K., Madi, Brenna, Iman, Juliann, Erin, Claire, Mandee, Charlotte, Devon, Patricia, Jasmine, Kim, Tara, Eileen, Sydni, Mary Ellen, Elisabeth, Elina, Megan, Emily C., Alyssa and Melanie: Thank you for all the photos, thoughtful feedback and, most of all, your willingness to take time out of your lives and schedules to make pies, especially in the sweltering summer heat.

To my editor, Rebecca. No words can adequately express the gratitude I owe to you and Page Street Publishing for making a lifelong dream come true. You made me an author and I'll be forever grateful for that.

To The Beatles, Fleetwood Mac, Nick Drake, Coldplay, Bon Iver, Washed Out, Jamie Cullum, Nick Mulvey, Mac DeMarco, José González, Fleet Foxes, Cocteau Twins, Ólafur Arnalds, Iron & Wine and all the musical artists that fuel my time spent in the kitchen and the studio: You ignite my creativity and inspire me infinitely. Thank you for scoring the soundtrack of my life.

To my All Purpose Flour Child community: You made this book possible. Thank you from the bottom of my heart for following along in my cooking journey with me and making my recipes. I hope this book inspires and empowers you to enjoy time spent in the kitchen, work with your hands, feed those you love and make more pie!

"AND IN THE END, THE LOVE YOU TAKE
IS EQUAL TO THE LOVE YOU MAKE."
-THE BEATLES

ABOUT THE AUTHOR

A PNW native, Taylor is a food stylist, recipe developer and photographer based in Seattle. Her work has been featured by *Red Magazine, Imbibe, Lenox,* Starbucks.com, *My Domaine, Bake from Scratch* and many others. In addition to shooting freelance photography and developing recipes for clients, she created the blog All Purpose Flour Child, where she shares highly seasonal and approachable recipes that inspire readers to get more joy out of time spent in the kitchen. Her kitchen table is always overflowing with a project, her speakers are usually blaring '70s rock and there's always a fine dusting of flour on her countertops. This is her debut cookbook.

INDEX